A POCKET BOOK ON
500
HOUSEHOLD
HINTS

JEAN McGLONE

octopus

Contents

First published 1983 by
Octopus Books Limited
59 Grosvenor Street
London W1

© 1983 Octopus Books Limited

Reprinted 1985

ISBN 0 7064 1926 X

Produced by Mandarin Publishers Ltd
22a Westlands Road, Quarry Bay, Hong Kong

Illustrations by Mike Watts

SECTION ONE
HOUSEHOLD SUPERSAVERS

3

Clever Budgeting

Income and expenditure	Keep a monthly or weekly record of what you spend. Keep all receipts, cheque stubs and any correspondence you may have had with shops about items you have bought or complaints you have made. If you get an increase in salary or the mortgage payments increase or decrease, then make a note of these in your budget and adjust your spending or saving appropriately.
Cash	Don't carry around more cash with you than you need – avoid temptation.
Credit	When you buy something on credit ask the shop for the true annual interest rate – one shop may charge you considerably more than another. Shops and stores with their own credit cards also have varying interest rates. Look out for the very few shops which actually give you interest on this type of budget account. Limit your hire purchase or credit commitments to no more than two items at a time, and preferably one.
Bank accounts	Always have two bank accounts – your normal current account and another special budget account for regular household bills into which you pay a set amount each month. Try to have a third one for savings, too! Banks all have different charges for accounts and different minimum balances for free banking. So before you open an account ask each bank about its charges.
Insurance	Shop around before taking out a home insurance policy. There are variations in both the cost and the type of cover available.

Extra income	Any extra money you earn from overtime or part-time casual jobs should be treated as extra rather than basic income. You will then be less likely to feel the pinch if overtime is cut.
Checking bills	Check that you have not been overcharged at the supermarket and that you have been given the correct amount off on any special offer items. Assistants can and do make mistakes.
Coupons	Take advantage of all the money-off coupons which appear in advertisements, on the backs of food packets or arrive in the mail.
Sizes	Make sure you know your family's correct measurements and the sizes of your household equipment so that you can buy the right size every time.
Servicing	Check very carefully what service and maintenance a firm offers with the appliances it sells. The cost of maintenance contracts on washing machines, freezers and so on varies from one firm to another, so shop around.
Fabric care	Look at the care labels on garments before you buy to make sure they provide long-term value for money. When buying fabric by the metre ask the assistant what its wash and wear properties are. Often there are no labels to tell you this on fabric.
Tinned food	Don't go for the very expensive brands of canned food. In the fruit department especially you can find that something half the price is just as good.
Remnants	Pick up remnants of fabric from the odds and ends counters of fabric shops and turn them into simple clothes for the children.

Food

Save money by reducing your consumption of convenience foods (frozen foods in particular can be very expensive compared to fresh) and bake and cook more yourself. Grow vegetables and fruit in the garden.

Cleaning bills

Save on dry cleaners' bills by choosing washable clothes and furnishings as far as possible.

Gadgets

Think twice about buying items such as knife sharpeners and other kitchen gadgets – the chances are that you will use your chip maker a few times and then go back to cutting the potatoes by hand because a knife is easier to wash.

Washing-up liquid

In spite of what the television advertisements say it is not always true that expensive washing-up liquids are better value because they are stronger. Size can often play a large part in value and tests have shown that a cheaper liquid in much larger sizes can be far better value than an expensive one.

Car sharing

If a friend or neighbour makes the same trip to work as you do then try to work out a car sharing arrangement, cutting the cost of travel. Also work out a rota with friends for collecting the children from school or other activities.

Economy tips

Cards
Don't put old greetings cards into the wastepaper basket. Keep them by the telephone and in the kitchen as they are ideal for making notes.

Paper
Keep old brown paper, gift wrapping paper and tissue paper and iron it with a steam iron. It can then be used again.

Batteries
Batteries in a torch or radio which have become weak can be given a new lease of life by setting them on top of a radiator for several hours – the heat does the trick.

Toothbrushes
Don't throw out old toothbrushes. The hard-bristled ones can be very useful for cleaning awkward corners in metal objects and the soft-bristled ones are ideal for dusting in crevices and corners.

Powder paints
Ordinary wallpaper paste (not the fungicidal types) can be mixed with children's powder paints. It will make the paint go further and will give a thicker texture, too.

Ice cream containers
Large plastic ice cream containers have all sorts of uses when empty. You can pack small items, such as fruit, into them and keep them in the freezer. They also make good containers for sandwiches to take on picnics and are handy in the kitchen, garage or workshop for storage. They can even be pressed into service on occasion to hold cakes and biscuits.

Salt containers
Plastic salt containers – both square and round – make excellent containers for dried goods in the kitchen. Put a band of brightly coloured sticky plastic round the middle part of a container and letters on the front.

Sweet jars

Persuade your local confectioner to give you those large plastic sweet jars when empty. They can be useful and decorative for holding household clutter, such as buttons, scraps of material or spare balls of knitting wool, and ideal in the children's room for holding jigsaw puzzles, building bricks and so on.

Milk cans

Anyone with a young baby may well accumulate milk cans. Don't throw them out – glue the lids on firmly, paint the cans with non-toxic paint in bright colours and stencil a number on the side of each one. The result is a set of bright and easy to handle blocks for a toddler to play with.

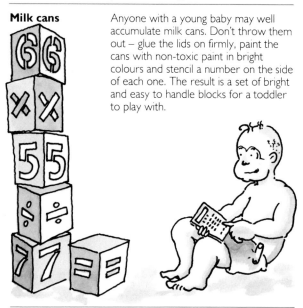

Screw-top jars

Use old screw-top jars underneath a shelf to store kitchen items or nails and other small items in the garage. Simply attach the lid to the underside of the shelf. The jar can then be screwed into it and suspended there. Unscrew to get at the contents.

Detergent containers

If you buy your detergent in bulk, keep the containers and turn them into drawers to hold odds and ends in the workshop. Simply lay them flat and cut out one side. The handle can be used as a drawer handle.

Oven gloves

Separate an unwanted pair of oven gloves, hemming the raw edges where you have cut, and use the individual gloves for dirty jobs around the house such as cleaning shoes or raking the ashes. The gloves can easily be popped into the washing machine for cleaning.

Knitting yarn

Don't ever buy what seems to be a bargain of cheap yarn for knitting, without buying a pattern for that particular yarn. The garment may not work out the right size if you use a pattern designed for a different yarn. To prepare old wool from a garment you have unravelled for re-knitting, wind the old yarn straight from the garment on to stiff card or a similar material. Press it with a steam iron: this will remove the wrinkles and kinks.

Elbow patches

When you knit garments for the children knit two oblong patches with the same wool and stitch these on to the elbows. This will help to prevent holes, but when the patches do wear through, simply unstitch them and the wool underneath will be new: thus you get double the wear.

Collars

When a shirt collar frays but the shirt is still good, remove the collar, reverse it and sew it back on.

Trousers

Trousers with wide flares which have gone out of fashion can very easily be converted to straight-legged ones. Take in the seams at both outside and inside leg, making sure that the seam lines are parallel.

Lampshades

Lampshades can become worn or just plain boring. Remove the fabric carefully and use it as a pattern to make another cover in whatever fabric appeals to you. You could match the shade cover to other soft furnishings.

9

Washing-up liquid bottles

Empty washing-up liquid bottles can provide the children with a game of skittles for practically no cost. Scrub off the lettering with some wire wool, take off the coloured top which dispenses the liquid and put some sand, beans or gravel inside the container to give it weight. Seal the top with plasticine and paint the bottle in bright stripes with household paint. Line them up in the garden or indoors and let the children knock them down with a rubber ball. The top of a washing-up liquid or bleach bottle, cut off just below the point where the sides begin to go straight down, makes an ideal funnel for pouring out liquids in the garage, or for pouring paint into a container.

Cleaning silver

There is no need to buy special dusters to clean and polish silver. Wash and dry old powder puffs and use them instead.

Cleaning clothes

Save cleaning bills by getting the dust off your clothes regularly. Use the vacuum cleaner on heavy items such as coats.

Shoes

If your shoes are looking dull and you have run out of shoe polish, any neutral colour of furniture or floor polish will be a good substitute.

Using the last drops

To get the last drop out of a bottle of hand lotion turn it upside down for several hours to allow all the liquid to run down. To get the last out of a tube of hand cream, cut open the plastic and you will be amazed to see how much cream is still lurking in the corners.

Barbecues

If you would like a barbecue in your back garden but cannot afford to buy one, make one with ordinary bricks. Build them up into a four-sided box shape and put a grill on top. You could use the wire shelves from your oven or grill pan or even a baking tray.

Candles

To use up any old candle ends which you cannot safely burn, turn them into floor polish. Melt down the candles and when the liquid is warm remove the bits of wick. Add turpentine in equal proportion to the melted candle – warm slightly before using. Make this in a container standing in or over hot water, NEVER stand it over a naked flame.

China

If you like a particular pattern of china then consider buying extras or replacements a lot more cheaply from the seconds in that particular design. There will be small imperfections in the glaze but check where they are. Sometimes they are hardly noticeable so the china is well worth buying.

Compost

Compost for pot plants is expensive, so eke it out this way. Put a layer of stones into a 35 cm (14") tub, then put in a few sheets of crumpled newspaper. Top this up with compost and you'll find your geraniums will still bloom happily in this throughout the summer.

Plant pots

Special pots for indoor plants are costly, so buy a large, ordinary plant pot, paint it white, stick on a transfer or a similar decoration and you have a cheap and decorative indoor pot.

Oil lamps

If you still have an old-fashioned oil lamp with an incandescent mantle you will know how fragile the mantle is. To strengthen it and make it last longer soak it in a tumbler of vinegar for a few minutes and dry thoroughly before using.

Lists

When you go shopping never go without a list. Make a careful note of all you need and stick to that – an impulse buy, however cheap, isn't a bargain if you don't need it, and rarely use it.

Jeans
Don't throw out jeans just because they are worn. Use iron-on patches, or simply make your own patches from any spare denim material.

Leather patches
If you like leather patches on clothes to give extra wear it may be cheaper, if you use them regularly, to buy a skin of washable leather and make your own. The cost will be much less, but it is only a money saver if you use a lot of patches. It might be worth sharing the cost of a skin with friends or neighbours who also want patches.

Table mats
To make your own table mats, buy a small piece of tweed remnant, cut it into rectangles or squares and make a fringe round the edges. You now have a set of cheap but attractive mats.

Sheets
If sheets begin to wear thin in the middle, cut them down lengthwise, sew the original selvedges together and machine stitch a hem round the new edges.

Roller blinds
Make your own roller blinds to match your decor. Most curtain fabrics are suitable, and can be stiffened with a special spray.

Curtains
Curtains are expensive to buy ready made or to have made up. But if you aren't confident enough to make your own you may still be able to save quite a bit of money by buying two bedspreads and hanging them as curtains if your windows are roughly the right size. Buy one to use on the bed, too, and you have a luxury look for very little.

Cushions
If you stain or mark part of a plain cushion cover, embroider a motif on to the stained area with some yarn or embroidery silk.

Blankets

If the edges of your blankets begin to fray, there is probably no need to think of buying new ones. Buy wide satin ribbon and bind round the edges of the blankets – they will be as good as new.

Face cloths

Face cloths can be fiddly. It is better to buy two and sew them together to make a mitt which is much easier to use in the bath.

Soap

Soap on a rope is ideal for a shower, but very expensive in the shops. Put your own soap on a rope for a fraction of the cost. Use your normal brand and put a hole through it – a skewer or a small-headed screwdriver will do the job. Slip a piece of nylon piping cord through the hole, knot it so that the cord can't slip back and there you are. Loose soaps are usually far better value than boxed or wrapped ones.

The last bit of a bar of soap is not much use for washing hands and tends to be thrown out. But collect all those ends, melt them down together over a gentle heat and press into a mould such as the bottom of a cottage cheese carton and you have a new bar of soap. Or add water and make a carton of soap jelly.

Cleaning liquid

Make your own cleaning liquid for furniture (good for removing sticky marks). Mix together one tablespoon of turpentine, three tablespoons of linseed oil and 1 litre (2 pints) of hot water. Stir well and allow to cool. Bottle and use as required on a soft cloth and rub over the furniture. Dry with another cloth and rub gently to a shine.

Storage under beds

If your bed does not happen to have drawer units below it you can still use the space to stow stuff away neatly if you buy the kind of wire trays used to hold paperwork and files in offices. They can go neatly under the bed and have the advantage of the contents being visible through the mesh.

Flower vases

If you are stuck for a flower container there is an alternative to the milk bottle! Turn an empty plastic bottle into a smart vase. Cut off the shaped top and then weight the bottom with some sand or stones to ensure that the container won't topple over. Spray it with gold or silver paint or cover it with a plastic self-adhesive material.

Hair care

If you find hair conditioner a rather expensive item, or you run out of it, just add a few drops of bath oil, baby oil or olive oil to the last rinsing water. And if you find the shampoo bottle empty use a mild washing-up liquid instead.

Value for money

Is the smallest can or packet always dearest and the largest always cheapest? No – in many cases the medium size works out the cheapest because it is usually the most popular seller. It is always worth checking it mathematically.

How to cut heating costs

Lofts and tanks

Insulate your loft and lag your hot water tank. If you cannot afford the proper insulation materials for the tank then use any old carpet felt or blankets that you have. Anything is better than no insulation at all.

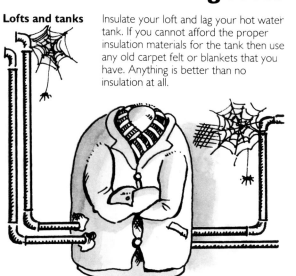

Pipes

Take a trip up to the attic or down to the cellar and check that all your pipes below ground floor or above top floor ceiling levels are properly wrapped, especially at the joints. Carpet felt wound round in strips will do the trick if commercially prepared materials are not available.

Radiators

Put foil – either the radiator foil or ordinary household foil – down behind your radiators, sticking it to the wall. This will help reflect the heat back into the room.

Radiator valves

Try to install individual thermostatic valves in every room. This way the temperature can be adjusted to each room.

Doors and windows

Draught-proof doors and windows by putting sealing strips into the frames.

15

Curtains

Use a special insulating material which you can buy by the metre to line curtains. Always have curtains long enough to tuck behind a radiator at the window as this prevents the heat going out of the window. Put your hand behind the curtains and you will see how cold it can be there and how great the heat loss could be.

Thermostats

Adjust your room thermostats in the spring and autumn. Try wearing warmer clothes occasionally instead of turning up the heat. If you can reduce the temperature in a room by just over 1°C over the winter you could cut your heating bills by more than 7%.

Unused rooms

Don't heat unused rooms and don't leave doors into them open. However, you should not let the temperature drop below 10°C as the main structure could suffer.

Lining paper

If you plan to redecorate a room it might be worth lining the walls first with polystyrene paper which can be bought by the roll. You can put decorative wallpaper on top.

Water heaters

Don't use your electric immersion heater using full price electricity to get hot water if you can get your water heated by your central heating system.

Heating times

Do time the heating boiler to switch off some while before you go to bed and put the clock further back as the weather gets warmer. Set the timer to come on later in the mornings, too.

Coal efficiency

Coal will burn much longer if sprinkled with a solution of water and washing soda in the proportion of 2.5 litres (4 pints) of water to a small handful of soda. The coal must be allowed to dry thoroughly before it can be used.

SECTION TWO
HOMECARE & DECORATING

17

Furniture and floors

Bruised wood

If you have bruises on furniture try applying a damp piece of rag to the area and then placing a hot iron over this – the resulting hot moisture and steam should swell the crushed wood and restore it. It may be necessary in bad cases to repeat the process several times. You can equally well use two thicknesses of dampened brown paper instead of a cloth.

Marks and stains

If you have a mark on the surface of a piece of furniture then take a piece of very fine grade steel wool and gently rub off the polish. Then go over the area with a proprietary stain product and polish as usual. White marks can sometimes be removed with camphorated oil.

Making wax polish

The basis of most wax polish is beeswax. This is available in lump form and allows you therefore to make your own polish. Shred the beeswax into a container, pour turpentine on to the wax and place the container in a pan of hot water. NEVER put the container over a flame. The precise amount of turpentine is not important, but the mixture when cool should be the consistency of butter in summertime. More turpentine can always be added. Keep in a closed tin.

'Antique' wax polish

If you want to give an antique effect to wood make your own wax polish as described, but add lamp-black powder while the mixture is still in a molten state. This turns it black and when applied to wood, leaves a black deposit in the grain and in corners.

Dusters

Old nylon tights (washed) make marvellous dusters to give a shine to wood.

Parquet floors	If you have a parquet floor which has been darkened by an accumulation of dirt and polish, the moving of furniture and general wear and tear, just wash off all the old polish with warm soapy water and then repolish. If it still seems discoloured it may be wise to use a little bleach in the water. A parquet floor which is badly worn is best scraped right down to the bare wood, sealed and then repolished.
Fading	If a piece of furniture becomes faded through exposure to the sun it should be rubbed down with a fine glasspaper, not down to the bare wood but about halfway through the body of the polish. It should then be treated with a tinted polish.
French polish	French polish can be bought, but you can also make your own by using 140-170 g (5-6 oz) of shellac dissolved in 0.5 litre (1 pint) of methylated spirits (rubbing alcohol).
Veneers	If you have veneered furniture which gets a lot of sunlight, give it extra protection to avoid cracks. Rub the wood occasionally with a silk cloth dipped in warm linseed oil. This should prevent cracks and blisters forming.
Protection against scratches	To prevent ornaments or vases scratching furniture, stick pieces of felt material to the bottom of them.

Carpets

Spreading the wear	With fitted carpets change the position of furniture fairly often to equalize the traffic lanes. Turn carpet squares regularly at least every six months. Allow an extra half metre on your stair carpet to enable it to be moved every six months.

British carpet classification scheme

Grade 1	Light domestic – for bedroom use.
Grade 2	Medium domestic – for bedrooms or other lightly-used rooms.
Grade 3	General domestic and/or medium contract use – general use.
Grade 4	Heavy domestic and/or general contract use – for anywhere in the home.
Grade 5	Heavy contract use.
Grade L	Luxury use – similar to grade 2 for wear but mainly for comfort and appearance.

Check the label on the back of the carpet before buying and you will find details of the classification on the label.

Choosing the right quality

Never be tempted by the colour of a carpet alone. Always check what grade it is in relation to where in the house it will be used. Remember that in general cheap carpeting will not give durability.

Carpet protection

Fit casters to all furniture to protect the carpets and put caster cups underneath. Put rugs down at the most vulnerable areas, especially in front of seating units where scuffing is likely to be at its worst.

Stairs

Make sure the stairpads cover the edge of the stair by at least 2½ cm (1").

Deep-pile carpets

If you have a deep-pile carpet with a shaggy texture then vacuuming is not enough. To prevent matting it must be raked as well with a special rake available from carpet shops.

Restoring colour

To restore a faded carpet, brush it well, put a tablespoon of common salt and 0.125 litre (¼ pint) of vinegar into a bucket of hot water and rub the carpet well with the solution. This will restore the colour and remove any greasy marks.

Heavy wear   Never skimp on quality when it comes to buying a carpet for the hall of a house. This gets much more wear than many people realise and it is essential to choose a hard-wearing quality carpet.

New carpets   Treat new carpets very gently. For the first month clean only lightly with a hand brush and then vacuum as normal.

Treating stains Animal or child 'accidents' on the carpets require speedy action. First remove the excessive moisture with a dry cloth and then sponge with lukewarm water. Some stains will respond to a solution of one teaspoon of white vinegar to three of warm water. Leave to dry and then apply a little detergent, dry again and vacuum. Grease or oil marks should be removed with carbon tetrachloride.
Blood should be sponged with cold water (hot water sets the stain) and then sponged with soapless detergent. Tea or coffee stains should be blotted up with tissues and then treated with detergent.
Red wine should be mopped up as quickly as possible. Blot up as much as you can with tissues or lavatory paper. Make up a solution of 1 teaspoon of liquid detergent and 1 teaspoon of white vinegar to 0.25 litre (½ pint) of warn, water. Work into the stain and dry with tissues. Keep working in this way until all traces are removed, drying very carefully after each application.

Moths   If you find there are moths in a carpet which has been rolled up in the attic, unroll it, wet a towel and put this over the affected part. Press with a hot iron until the towel is dry. The steam and heat will destroy moths and eggs.

Rugs   To prevent rugs slipping on polished floors stitch foam strips to the back.

21

Laundry

Net curtains

Net curtains can be washed inside a pillowcase to prevent machine damage.

Flameproof finishes

Soap powder can damage a flameproof finish so check that the powder is suitable for flame-resistant fabrics before using.

Never soak items made of silk, wool, leather or fabrics with a flame-resistant finish.

If static electricity is a problem in your clothes then use a fabric conditioner on the material in the wash.

Wool items

Never rub woollen sweaters which need to be hand-washed – friction is what causes shrinkage and pilling. So wash gently, moving the garment as little as possible. A garment will hold its shape better if you do up any buttons before washing. If the ribbing at neck and bottom and cuffs looks as though it might stretch, then run a thread through it and gather before washing.

When you have rinsed woollies squeeze them – don't wring out. But you can give a three-second spin just to get the excess water out without damage. Then coax carefully into shape and dry flat. Finally, steam iron if you feel it's necessary. Fold a sweater the way the wool industry does: lay it face down, pick up one sleeve and fold it back along the length, taking a third of the sweater with it. Do the same with the other sleeve tucking in protruding cuffs. Double the sweater over and put into a plastic bag.

Wash any woollen garment inside out to prevent pilling and use mild soapflakes.

A woollen tea cosy will retain its shape if after washing you place it over a teapot filled with boiling water. It will help it dry quickly, too.

Dyeing

Preparation

Wash all fabrics before you dye them. With new fabrics wash to remove any dressing they may have as this could prevent dye penetration. If a fabric is stained remove the stains first before dyeing with the special solution available for that purpose. If you want to change the colour completely and the fabric is too dark to take a new lighter colour then first take out all the original colour with a special stripper.

Dyeing in the washing machine

Do not try to dye a full load in your washing machine. Put in only half your usual load to allow plenty of room for circulation.

Run a little bleach and water through the rinse cycle on your washing machine after dyeing to take away all traces of colour.

Always put some salt in the water as it helps the colour to set.

Washing dyed fabrics

Always wash items you have dyed separately. Do not use bleaches or biological detergents on dyed fabrics.

Matching thread

Always remember when you are dyeing any fabric, whether furnishing or clothes, to tack in some white thread. This will dye at the same time and you can then take out the tacking and put the thread in your sewing box. You will have an exact match when repairs are needed.

Paper

You can tie-dye tissue paper to make really special wrapping paper for gifts. All you do is pleat, fold or furl the paper into triangles, bind with string at intervals, stand the tied paper on edge in shallow cold-water dye until it begins to seep into the folds. Drip dry, then dye the opposite edge in a contrasting or blending colour.

23

Faded linen	Give faded pillowcases, tablecloths, napkins and other such items a new lease of life with cold-water dye. They can be dyed to match new decorative schemes.
Tie-dyeing	An old cotton rug can be tie-dyed with cold dyes to produce a Scandinavian look. Tie the rug at intervals diagonally with some string and then rinse and dry in the usual way.
Candles	To dye plain household candles – melt some stearin (from craft shops) in a ratio of one part stearin to ten parts dye. Add cold dye to the stearin in a saucepan, stirring well. Melt paraffin wax or household candles in a saucepan, removing the wicks, and add the dye solution. Heat to 82°C, stirring constantly. Pour the mixture into old yogurt pots. When the wax is rubbery, bore a hole in the middle with a knitting needle and insert a length of waxed wick, then seal with wax so that the wick is firmly set in.

To dye or not to dye

Fabrics you can dye
Acetate, Alaston, Bri-nylon, Canvas, Celon, Cotton, Crimplene, Dacron, Dacron/Cotton, Darelle, Delustra, Dicel, Diolen, Enkalon, Enkasheer, Evlan, Helanca, Lancofil, Lancola, Lancolene, Lansil, Linen, Lycra, Nylon, Perlon, Raycelon, Sarille, Shareen, Silk, Spanzelle, Tendrelle, Tergal, Terlenka, Terylene, Terylene/Cotton, Trevira, Tricel, Tricelon, Vincel, Viscose Rayon, Wool, Zantrel.
All can take multi-purpose (hot water) or liquid dyes. Some also can take cold-water dyes.

Fabrics you cannot dye
Acrilan, Cashmilon, Courtelle, Dralon, Fibreglass, Leacril, Neospun, Orlon, Sayelle or any specially treated fabrics such as those with a drip-dry finish.
All the acrylics, glassfibres and tricels are included in this category.

Sewing box

Buttons

After sewing buttons on a garment dot the thread with colourless nail varnish to help the buttons stay on longer.

When cutting a button off a garment it is very easy to snip into the fabric by mistake. To avoid doing so slip a hairpin between the button and the cloth, put your scissors above the pin and cut.

Use special button or carpet thread to sew buttons on heavy fabrics when extra strength is needed – on jackets for instance.

Buttons on coats, outer jackets, mackintoshes, etc., undergo heavy strain and need reinforcing. To do this place a small piece of fabric directly under the button location on the inside of the garment and sew through this when attaching the button. The same technique can be used for very delicate fabrics that are likely to tear.

It can sometimes be very difficult to find all the matching buttons in a set by searching through your button tin or box. So take a spare evening to tie each set of buttons together by threading a piece of cotton through them and tying it. And if you throw out a garment always take off the buttons and tie them together before getting rid of it.

If you cannot find any buttons in the shade you need dye plain white buttons with a hot-water dye.

Darning

If you find darning the heels of socks tricky and you don't have a darning mushroom, borrow one of the children's small rubber balls and push it inside the sock to give you a firm surface to work against. When darning worn bed or table linen, tack a piece of muslin behind the worn part, making it easier to darn across with the sewing machine.

25

Zips

If the teeth in a zip break near the bottom you can still keep using it for a short time. Make a temporary repair by taking a strong matching thread and sew across the zip with a double thickness several times. That way the zip will not go beyond the point where you have stitched. Some zips simply won't stay shut because they do not have a special tooth at the top. To cure this problem stitch on a very small button near the top of the zip and put a small loop of double-twisted thread through the hole in the zip pull. You can then hook it over the button once the zip is closed.

Small scissors

Always store small scissors with a cork pressed on to the tips, to prevent damage to other items.

Picking up pins

If you drop pins and they scatter over a wide area a magnet will pick them up quickly and efficiently.

Double-sided items

If stitching a repair on any double-sided item, such as a cushion cover or pocket, then put a piece of thick card or plastic inside it. This will prevent you stitching both sides of it together.

Piping cord

Always wash piping cord before use.

Curtains	To give your curtains a really graceful hang use lead-weighted curtain tape inside the hems, being careful to use the weight of tape suitable to the fabric. On full length curtains make sure the hem is about an inch above the floor level to allow the curtains to hang properly and prevent the material wearing quickly as a result of rubbing and chafing. This also applies to shorter curtains with a wide window sill below them. If you move house and find that your favourite curtains are not long enough to fit your new windows you may be able to solve the problem if you have any spare material left over. Add an extra section to the bottom and then hide the seam by stitching a plain braid over it to pick up one of the colours in the materials.
Pressing pile fabrics	Don't ruin the pile in a fabric by careless pressing. Press the material face down over several layers of damp towelling. Don't touch the iron to the fabric but just let the steam penetrate.
Pressing alterations	To remove creases or iron-shine from areas on a garment which has been altered apply white vinegar with a brush and then steam press the area.
Cord ends	Any ends of cord on curtains or cushions which are liable to fray should be given a quick touch of nail varnish.
Fraying	Use a fine hair spray along fraying edges of difficult material when making it up.
Lengthening sleeves	If your child has outgrown the sleeves of his jacket you can sew on knitted cuffs to give extra length.
The crease test	Before you buy any fabric give it a quick crease test – just crunch a corner of it in your hand, let it go and see if the creases fall out quickly. If they remain be wary.

Stains

Tea and coffee	For washable fabrics, rinse in warm water, soak in a weak ammonia solution and rinse again. For non-washables, rub in a little glycerine, leave for an hour, then sponge with warm water.
Milk	Soften with glycerine if the stains are old, leave ten minutes and then rinse in warm suds.
Egg	Soak washable fabrics in cold salt water, then sponge with warm suds. Leave to dry and apply carbon tetrachloride. For non-washables, apply salt water, leave to dry and then sponge lightly.
Fruit	Sprinkle with salt and leave for a few minutes before washing. For upholstery, use liquid detergent and then a little methylated spirits (rubbing alcohol).
Make-up	Lift or scrape off as much as possible and then wash as usual.
Alcoholic drinks	Rinse washable fabrics in tepid water. For old stains on cotton or linen moisten with I part glycerine to 2 parts water and then soak in cold water. For non-washable fabrics dab on a warm borax solution.
Chocolate	Wash normally. For non-washable fabrics apply carbon tetrachloride then leave to dry.
Tar	Scrape as much as possible off first then treat with carbon tetrachloride. Remove any residue with methylated spirits.
Nail polish	Spillages may be removed from fabrics by sponging off with nail polish remover and then washing in warm water. DO NOT use remover on acetate fabrics such as Tricel as it will damage them.

Mildew
Soak the article in milk overnight and the next day place it in the sun to dry. Another method is to spread soft soap mixed with starch, salt and the juice of a lemon over the mildew on both sides of the fabric. Again place in the sun for a day to dry. Whites can be soaked in 1 part bleach to 100 parts water with 1 tablespoon of vinegar added.

Medicine
Make up a paste of fuller's earth, leave to dry and brush off.

Beat-the-stain kit

With the following items you should be able to lead an unblemished life and cope with the stains on furnishings and clothes that happen in any home. Always keep substances away from children.

Ammonia
A solvent used to neutralise acid stains. Do not use on silk, wool, aluminium or sisal. Use 1 part to 4 parts water.

Methylated spirit (rubbing alcohol)
Another solvent for grease and acid stains.

Borax
A mineral salt that is slightly antiseptic and both softens and bleaches. Use for tannin stains. 1 teaspoon to 0.5 litre (1 pint) water.

Glycerine
A lubricant and solvent which must be washed off with water.

Carbon Tetrachloride
An all-purpose cleaner for grease. Dangerous when used with rubber.

Hydrogen peroxide
A solvent which should be used in the proportion of 1 part to 10 parts water. When using solvents put a pad of absorbent cotton wool below the stain and apply the liquid with another pad from above. Change pad when soiled, then wash fabric as usual.

Ink

To remove ink stains from coloured material make a paste of dry mustard and water, spread over the mark and leave for 15 minutes. Wash and rinse. For white fabrics moisten with salt and lemon juice and hold over steam. For ballpoint pen marks use warm suds and methylated spirits. Red ink should be soaked in a borax solution. Felt-pen marks should be treated with a hard soap wash and then methylated spirits.

Rust

To remove rust marks from fabrics coat thickly with cream of tartar, put the item into a pan of hot water and leave for a few minutes. This can only be done with washable fabrics.

Chewing gum

Apply an ice cube to harden the gum, then scrape it off and wash the fabric. For non-washable fabrics try carbon tetrachloride.

Scorch marks

Light scorch marks should respond to washing. Heavier ones should be soaked in glycerine, then washed and any remaining traces removed with a solution of one part hydrogen peroxide to ten parts of water. On coloured wool, slightly rubbing the marks with the edge of a silver coin works wonders.

Damp

Stains on linen can be rubbed with finely powdered chalk, treating each mark separately. Leave on the linen until dry and then wash the material.

Marking ink

To remove marking ink from linen immerse in a solution of chloride of lime, in a few minutes the marks will gradually go white, because a new substance called chloride of silver has been formed. This white chloride is soluble in liquid ammonia, so remove the linen quickly and put it into ammonia for a few minutes only, then rinse with clean water.

Grass stains   Sponge with methylated spirits and then wash in the usual manner.

Soot   Ordinary salt is the best thing to use if soot from the chimney falls on to the carpet. Just sprinkle it on and leave for a short time then vacuum up the salt.

Candle grease   To remove candle grease from clothing scrape off what you can then place a piece of blotting paper on each side of the fabric and press with a hot iron. Any traces still left can be taken off with a little carbon tetrachloride.

Blood   To remove recent bloodstains soak in cold water to which you have added salt and then wash. For older stains, give the salt treatment and then add a few drops of ammonia to the washing water. On upholstery, sponge with cold salt water, apply a paste of cold cornflour, leave it to dry and then brush off.

Stains on kitchenware

Coffee and tea pots   Put a tablespoon of washing soda in the pot, fill with boiling water, leave for an hour and wash thoroughly.

Enamelware   Rub with cut lemon sprinkled with salt.

Aluminium   Boil some rhubarb in it. The acid will remove discoloration.

Glassware   Fill vases and decanters with water plus a teaspoon of ammonia, leave overnight and rinse. Treat sediment stains with 1 tablespoon salt to 0.125 litre ($\frac{1}{4}$ pint) vinegar.

Silver   Tarnished cutlery, if it can be immersed in boiling water, should be boiled in an aluminium pan with 14 g ($\frac{1}{2}$ oz) washing soda per litre of water. Simmer, wash in soapy water and rinse. Otherwise, use a neutral, liquid detergent.

Cleaning and renovating

Windows	There are many fluids you can buy for cleaning windows, but a good old-fashioned method which works well and costs little is to use plain water with a dash of vinegar in it. Apply with a chamois leather. Old newspapers used to give a final polish to your windows do a really marvellous job, but wear rubber gloves or you will get your fingers black with the newsprint.
Aluminium	A good method of cleaning aluminium is to rub it with soapy fine steel wool, using a circular movement.
Brass	If the usual methods of cleaning brass fail, try dipping the object into a bowl of Coca-Cola and watch how it brightens. Leave it to soak.
Bronze	After dusting bronze articles it is a good idea to rub them over with a soft cloth dipped in linseed oil.
Brushes	To wash household brushes and freshen them put a few drops of ammonia in boiling water. Dip the brushes, bristles downwards, in the water and out again, keeping the backs and handles free from water. Repeat until bristles are clean, rinse in cold water, shake and leave to dry
Straw matting	Straw mattings should be dusted regularly and washed occasionally with salt and water. The salt prevents them turning yellow. Bran water in the proportions of two handfuls bran to 4½ litres (1 gallon) water can also be used.
Suede	Shiny patches on suede shoes and gloves can be removed by rubbing very gently with a fine-grade emery paper and then steaming to raise up the pile.

Mincers   To clean a mincer put a few pieces of dry bread through it after use.

Sponges   To clean a sponge add a tablespoon of ammonia to 1 litre (2 pints) of boiling water. Put the sponge into this, let it soak for about an hour then squeeze it as dry as possible. Then change the water, adding just a teaspoon of ammonia to it and work the sponge about with your hands. Rinse in cold water. If the sponge is very slimy add some salt to the rinsing water.

Stone   If stone steps or window sills are stained add a little paraffin to hot soapy water and scrub the marks with this.

Umbrellas   Before using a new umbrella put a small amount of Vaseline into the hinge part of the frame. Vaseline will not spread and spoil the covering but will help prevent rust.

Oil paintings   Oil paintings can be freshened up if you rub a freshly cut slice of potato dampened in cold water over the surface. Dry and then polish with a piece of silk. The surface should then be rubbed over with a flannel very slightly dampened with linseed oil.

Straw hats

To brighten up a black straw hat, sponge with water and then sponge again with the beaten white of an egg to give a gloss and stiffen it. White straws should be cleaned by rubbing fuller's earth into the braid then shaking it out.

Velvet collars

A velvet collar can be renovated by rubbing gently with a cloth dipped in ammonia and water, but immediately after this, hold the collar over a hot iron to raise the pile.

Piano keys

If an ivory key on a piano has turned yellowish apply a mixture of equal parts of methylated spirits and water, using a squeezed-out pad of absorbent cotton wool.

Alabaster

To clean alabaster, sponge with a piece of soft flannel that has been dipped in a little turpentine and then in powdered pumice. Afterwards wash the item in warm soapy water in which you have dissolved a little borax. Dry and polish with a soft rag.

Wood furniture

Clean wooden furniture with warm water and vinegar (one tablespoon to 1 litre (2 pints) water), rub dry and then polish with a soft cloth. To remove ring marks and stains rub over the surface lightly with a very fine quality of steel wool, fill in with stain and apply polish.

Bamboo furniture

To clean bamboo furniture use a soft brush dipped in salt water. Dry with a soft cloth then rub over the surface with a very little linseed oil.

Bicycles

If you are storing a bicycle away for the winter it is a good idea to cover the metal parts with a little Vaseline and then turn the machine upside down to take the weight off the tyres. If the store room is very dry keep a basin of water in it.

Brick fireplaces Soot on brick fireplaces can be removed by applying diluted hydrochloric acid. This should only be used on the actual stains and then rinsed off thoroughly.

Skin rugs Animal skin rugs can be cleaned by rubbing over with hot bran, using the palms of the hands and working in a circular movement. The rug should be well shaken to remove all the bran.

Coral To keep coral clean, simply polish it with tissue paper. If very dirty it can be boiled in soapy water containing a little soda then dried and polished with a chamois leather.

Grouting Grouting in between ceramic tiles does get rather dirty. It can be cleaned with a solution of domestic bleach and water. Leave it on the surface for a few minutes, rinse off with clear water and then dry.

Furs Fuller's earth can be used for cleaning furs – sprinkle it in, leave to settle and shake it out.

Wallpaper Marks on wallpaper may be removed by rubbing a slice of bread gently against the paper. This is especially effective for soot marks near a fireplace. To remove a grease mark from wallpaper, make a thick paste from cleaning fluid and French chalk. Apply to the spot, leave overnight then brush off carefully, repeating if necessary.

Silk To renovate silk articles affected by dust, put the material flat on an ironing board or table and rub over every part of it with a piece of soft silk. If there is staining, dilute some pure alcohol with water, rub it gently into the material, turn it over and iron with a moderate iron.

35

Silk blouses

Silk blouses should be washed in warm soapy water and then rinsed. You can stiffen them with a solution of gum water made as follows: 28 g (1 oz) gum arabic (light-coloured) in 0.25 litre (½ pint) boiling water. Heat until dissolved then strain into a bottle and keep covered. Use 1 tablespoon of the mixture to 1 litre (2 pints) water. Allow the blouse to dry, put it flat on a clean cloth, spray with the solution, roll it up, leave for an hour then iron on the wrong side with a moderate iron.

Gold

A good way to polish gold articles is to take a small quantity of jeweller's rouge and mix it with a little oil to form a paste. Apply this with a piece of cotton wool until the required polish is obtained. The article should then be rinsed in hot soapy water and dried. Gold items can be rubbed up with a chamois which has a little jeweller's rouge in it. Clean gold plate by washing in warm soapy water, drying with a soft cloth and polishing with a chamois.

Lacquer

The best method of renewing the gloss on lacquered articles is to dip them in warm water containing a little sour milk or lemon juice. Dry in a warm place and then rub with a piece of cloth. Finally polish with a chamois.

Copper and brass

Lacquering is advisable on all copper and brass items that would otherwise need constant cleaning.

Japanning and papier mâché

To clean japanned and papier mâché articles sponge in lukewarm water, using a little soap if greasy. Dry thoroughly and polish first with a soft duster. Never let boiling water touch japanned trays as it will cause the varnish to peel off. Hot plates or dishes must have a stand under them or they will cause blisters and leave white marks.

Enamelware

Always buy good quality enamelware for cooking. Inferior enamel can chip and this is dangerous. Enamelware should be well scrubbed inside and out and then thoroughly rinsed in clean water. If pans are stained, rub them well with lemons sprinkled with salt from which the yellow rind and juice have been removed. If you burn an enamel pan, put in a tablespoon of vinegar, fill it with cold water and boil for ten minutes. Leave it to soak and you will then find that the charred food can be removed without using harsh abrasive.

Vellum lampshades

Old lampshades made of vellum should be kept pliable by rubbing over with a cloth moistened with linseed oil.

Diamonds

Diamonds can be washed with water and dried carefully with blotting paper. If you roll the paper to a point you can get into all the corners.

Oil and vinegar bottles	If oil and vinegar bottles have become discoloured they can be cleaned by adding tea leaves to a little water in the bottle. Gently drop in a ballbearing and swirl it round and round.
Felt hats	Felt hats may be given a general clean by rubbing over the surface with bran. This should then be completely removed with a soft brush.
Fingernails	If fingernails become stained or discoloured soak them in 0.5 litre (1 pint) of warm water to which you have added a teaspoon of lemon juice.
Marble	To clean marble put together a mixture consisting of equal parts of soft soap, quicklime and caustic potash. Apply with a brush and leave on the marble for several days after which it must be wiped off. To polish marble take 225 g (½ lb) of washing soda, 225 g (½ lb) each of powdered chalk and pumice stone. Sift these through a fine sieve and mix into a paste with water. Rub the paste over the marble, leave for a few hours, wash with soap and water and give a final polish.
Ostrich feathers	To dry clean and curl an ostrich feather hold it in sulphur fumes – this should be done in the open air. To dress an ostrich feather without curling it, make a soapy lather, dip the feather into it and then squeeze it gently between the fingers to eliminate the dirt. When it is quite clean it should be rinsed in cold water and then laid flat on a clean towel. The feather should then be dabbed rapidly with a soft handkerchief until the fronds are light and fluffy.
Leather upholstery	Shabby leather upholstery can be brightened up a little if it is wiped over with a cloth wrung out in water to which a little vinegar has been added.

Chamois gloves

Light chamois gloves can be cleaned by washing but may become hard. So make sure the washing and rinsing waters are lukewarm and have a few drops of olive oil added.

White kid gloves

White kid gloves, if only slightly soiled, can be rubbed with cream of tartar. For heavy soiling use a piece of rag dipped in carbon tetrachloride and allowed almost to dry before rubbing on the gloves. Afterwards the gloves should be rubbed with breadcrumbs until all the stains are removed.

Pigskin gloves

Pigskin gloves can normally be washed in the usual way and, when dry, a little French chalk should be rubbed in.

Chamois leather

Soak in 0.5 litre (½ pint) of soapy water to which three tablespoons of household ammonia have been added. The leather should then be worked about with a wooden spoon so as to press out as much dirt as possible. It should be rinsed in tepid water, rubbed well, finally rinsed in fresh water several times and hung out to dry in the shade. The leather should be pulled frequently to keep it soft.

Brown leather

To remove stains from brown shoes or boots cut a piece of lemon and rub it on well. Then polish with brown polish. A banana skin also acts as a good polish for brown boots and shoes.

Light tan leather

When light tan shoes become marked and worn-looking, darken the leather with a cloth dipped in ammonia to disguise the wear. Use even strokes and not too much liquid at the one time, to avoid streaking.

Patent leather

Keep patent leather shoes in good condition by cleaning with vaseline jelly. It adds months to their life.

Silk lace

Silk lace should be soaked in hot milk and borax to prevent it turning yellow. Lace when not in use should not be kept in white paper – blue paper should be used and the corners should be folded over so that the lace is quite covered.

Old lace

Old lace can be cleaned by steeping it in water in which borax has been dissolved. Wash out next day in soapy water and rinse several times. Then dip the lace into warm water to which a few lumps of sugar have been added and pin it out on to a cloth to dry. Really valuable lace should not be handled in this way – it can be folded up with dry powdered magnesia sprinkled between each fold and left for some days when the powder should have absorbed some of the dirt.

Gilt frames

To brighten gilt frames of any kind, take sufficient flowers of sulphur (available from pharmacists) to give a golden tinge to 1 litre (1½ pints) water, and in this water boil four or five bruised onions. Strain off the liquid and when cold use it to wash any gilding which needs restoring. Use a soft brush.

Copper

Copper utensils must be very thoroughly cleaned to avoid the formation of verdigris, which is a poisonous substance. Wash copper well in hot water, then with a piece of flannel rub on a mixture of salt, fine sand and vinegar. Wash the copper again in warm water so that all traces of vinegar are removed. Dry and polish. A little oil rubbed over the metal from time to time will keep it bright.

Linoleum

Never use abrasives when cleaning linoleum. The best thing to use is warm water with mild soap.

Vases

If you have a vase which is stained inside and you have found it impossible to clean by the usual methods, put some water in it, pop in a couple of denture-cleaning tablets and leave it to soak. Rinse out well.

Thermos flask

If a Thermos flask is not in daily use, store it with the stopper and cup removed. After use, always fill it with hot water to which a teaspoon of bicarbonate of soda has been added, then rinse thoroughly.

Lavatories

Never mix a bleach and a proprietary cleaner in the bowl as chlorine gas may be given off and it is highly toxic. Use one or the other.

Cushions

What do you do if the cat sits on your best cushion and brushing simply will not remove the hairs? Wind some lengths of Sellotape round your fingers, sticky side out – it will pick up the hairs easily.

Blocked sinks

Sink slightly blocked? A handful of washing soda put down the plug hole followed by boiling water should clear things and it will also keep the drain area clean and sweet.

41

Ceilings

Ceilings blackened by soot from the fire can be cleaned by sponging with water to which a piece of ordinary washing soda has been added.

Clothes lines and pegs

New clothes lines and pegs should be boiled before being used and wiped over regularly with a damp cloth to avoid marking clothes. If you put a hole through a sponge and thread one end of a washing line through it before attaching it to the pole you can then run the sponge along the line every time you use it to keep it clean.

Tea-leaf polish

Tea leaves kept for several days, infused with boiling water and then strained, make a useful polish costing nothing for mirrors, windows, glasses and varnished wood.

Ash

If you have an open fire use the ash to clean stubborn marks off tiles.

Protecting your hands

If you are doing a dirty job around the house and have neither rubber gloves nor barrier cream then rub some washing-up liquid on to your hands and down under your nails and let it dry on the skin. You will find it provides a protective coating which makes the dirt easier to wash off.

42

Repairs

Cisterns

If there is a drip in the lavatory cistern, take off the cover and lift the ball up with your hand. If the drip stops this may have been the cause, so gently bend the arm attached to the ball downwards very slightly – that should stop the drip.

Gloves

If you are mending the finger of a glove put one of the old-fashioned wooden clothes pegs with a round end into the finger and you will find it easier to stitch.

Climbing frames

If the children have a climbing tower in the garden it is a good idea to check all the nuts and bolts and screws at the joints to make sure they are tight and so avoid accidents. If any of the pipes or tubes have an open end stop it up with a plastic filler. This will prevent water getting in to rust the metal which might make it break.

Wallpaper

On damaged or torn wallpaper you can do an almost invisible repair with a spare piece. Never CUT a patch to fit – tear a piece with the edges uneven, and paste it into the damaged area. You will find that there are no hard edges round the patch but that it blends in with the old.

Carpet

To stop the cut edges of carpet fraying, lightly touch a little rubber-based white glue along the edge and it will stay firm. If someone stubs out a cigarette on your carpet or there is some other sort of small area of damage you can do a repair job yourself providing you can get rug wool in the right shade. Knot the wool through the back of the carpet as if you were rugmaking, then trim off the excess length on the right side of the carpet.

43

Net curtains

To repair torn sheer curtains apply a thin coat of colourless nail varnish to the tear, then press the edges together with your fingernails until dry. Next time you wash them however you must be careful not to pull or stretch the curtains too much.

Fuses

Always keep a selection of fuse wires and fuses in the sizes you need by the fuse box so that if a fuse goes you won't have to search around trying to find them. If you run out of either always replace them immediately.

Chairs

When using cane to do a repair to a chair, soak the cane in cold water first to make it pliable. When renewing webbing on a chair soak the webbing overnight in cold water and nail in position while still damp. It will dry taut and give better support.

Linoleum

To repair linoleum where the castor of a chair has damaged it, place a piece of fresh linoleum over the damaged piece, matching the pattern exactly. Then cover the patch with a large can lid and hammer it down on to the linoleum. You will hammer it into a shape exactly required to fit, because the lid will make a circle right through both old and new layers. You can then lift out the old circle and fit in the new.

Screws

If you are trying to put in a screw in an area above your head and find it keeps dropping out before you can actually start screwing it, put a little chewing gum in the hole first. This will hold the screw and give you a chance to get it in.
To remove a screw which has been sealed in with paint, place the tip of a hot soldering iron or red-hot poker on the screw head. This burns off the paint and expands the metal. Leave it to cool and then extract the screw.

Zinc pails

To make a temporary repair to a zinc pail, place a small piece of putty inside the pail and a large piece on the outside. Flatten them both out. When the putty has dried the pail will hold water.

Hinges

To cure squeaky hinges take a little oil and apply to the joint of each hinge, working the door back and forward. Wipe away any excess.

String

If you are using sttring and want a really tight job, wet the string first before you use it – it will dry taut.

Instant glue

If you use instant glue and get your fingers stuck together by mistake then don't panic. It is possible to separate them if you plunge your hands into warm soapy water and gently ease the skin apart.

Clean surfaces

If using glue to repair something in the house, make sure that the surfaces to be stuck are absolutely clean. Water, grease, dust and old adhesive can all cause failure and it may not be the fault of the glue at all.

Clamps

When sticking two surfaces together put some sort of clamping device on the join.

When can the item be used again?

No matter what the manufacturer's blurb says, it is wise to wait much longer than recommended before using the item being glued. Epoxies in particular can go on hardening for some time after they are supposed to have reached full strength.

Decorating

Samples
When you put new wallpaper or new curtains in a room it is a good idea to keep small samples together in a plastic bag. Then if you go to buy paint or accessories for the room take the bag of samples with you and matching will be easy.

Mould
If you find any mould on the walls when you are going to redecorate then this must be dealt with. Household bleach applied to the wall with a sponge will kill off the spores.

How much do you need?
To work out how much wallpaper you will need divide the height of your walls into the length of the roll. That will tell you how many lengths you will get from each roll. Then divide the width of the roll into the distance around the room for the total number of rolls needed.

Wallpaper storage
Always store rolls of wallpaper flat. Don't stand them on end or the edges may be damaged.

Soaking off old wallpaper
To soak off old vinyl wallpaper, rub over the paper with a pan scourer before applying the water to let it soak right through the plastic coat and take effect underneath.

Sizing
Always size walls with a coat of paste before starting. This is to seal porous walls which would absorb paste and not allow the paper to stick properly. The sealant also makes it easier to slide the paper on the wall when butting.

The paste brush
When pasting wallpaper tie thick string lightly across the top of the paste bucket and use this for resting your brush on between pastings. The same idea can be used for a paint can.

Blisters

If you do get bumps and blisters in wallpaper after it has dried then try this trick. Very, very carefully with a razor blade make a tiny incision into the bubble. Push in a little fresh paste and press the paper down – you won't notice the cut if you take care to do it cleanly.

Washing walls

To wash walls start from the bottom and work upwards. If you start at the top dirty water streaks will dry and paint may not disguise them.
Make sure surfaces are really clean before you apply paint. It simply will not stick to greasy surfaces, so wash with a mild detergent solution first. If there are greasy marks mop with white spirit and then wash with detergent before painting.

Roller trays

Line the paint roller tray with aluminium foil. You can simply throw it away when the job is finished and it will keep the tray free from a build up of hardened paint.

Brushes

Before you use a new brush to paint work it over a wall using clean water, to get all the loose hairs off the brush.

Sealing

Never paint straight on to bare wood as the paint will just soak into the porous surface. A sealing coat of primer is absolutely necessary first.

Thinning paint

When thinning paints remember that emulsion must always be thinned with water and gloss with white spirits. Don't thin non-drip paints.

Paint smells

To get rid of the smell of paint stand a bucket of water in which a few sliced onions are immersed in a newly painted room overnight and the smell will disappear.

Pasting

Always brush on wallpaper paste from the centre of the paper outwards, not from the edges in. The latter method may cause the paste to go underneath the edge and on to the right side of the paper.

Even if you are using a ready-pasted paper which only requires to be wet, mix up a small quantity of ordinary wallpaper paste and keep it to hand. There will probably be a few edges which won't stick down and you will need a small amount of paste for those.

Batches

If you haven't taken the precaution of buying sufficient paper for the job from the same batch, and you do look like running out, then try to complete one wall with the same lot and then start a new wall with a roll from a new one. Any difference in the colours will be far less noticeable that way.

Cutting off excess

If you have not cut your paper to exactly the right size and you have a margin, then wait until the paper is dry before cutting off excess with a very sharp knife or razor blade.

Skirting boards

Be careful when painting skirting boards that you don't get paint all over the floor. A double sheet of newspaper folded to a straight edge can be a great help – use it as a mask by pushing it well up to the area being painted to catch any drips. Rub off any splashes immediately.

Window frames

A mask can be very useful, too, when painting window frames. Put a piece of paper hard up against the frame where it meets the glass and stick it to the glass with Sellotape. Or put a strip of Sellotape against the frame on the surface of the glass and then pull it off when you have painted the frame and before the paint dries.

Doors

Doors can be tricky to paint and it can be very noticeable if you make a bad job of it. Remove any door handles or fitments before you start painting. Start at the top of the door, doing any mouldings or panels first, and then work systematically downwards. Apply the paint in a wide down-stroke and then run your brush up and down on the line. Always brush firmly down the line of the grain before going on to the next section.

Cleaning brushes

To clean a paint brush, make a hole through the handle and push a thin piece of stick or wire through it. You will then be able to suspend the brush in a jar of turpentine with the stick or rod resting on top of the jar. This will prevent the bristles from getting bent and they will also keep clear of any sediment which forms at the bottom. To clean old, hard, paintbrushes, stand them in a pan and cover the bristles with vinegar. Boil for 15 minutes then rinse in hot soapy water and give a final rinse in clear water. Allow to dry naturally.

Storing paint tins

When you store a half-finished paint can the best plan is to turn it upside down on the shelf. That way there is no airspace at the top of the can so that no skin will form, and when you want to use the can again it is a simple matter to turn it back the right way up. Alternatively, a little water poured on top of oil-based paints will exclude air and keep the paint liquid.

Areas round switches

Areas round light switches in a room tend to get grubby as fingers miss the switch and hit the wall instead. So after redecorating buy some self-adhesive transparent plastic and put this round the light switch. Then you can just wipe it down.

49

Electrical appliances

Choosing an iron

Remember that it is not the weight of it which is the most important factor. Do not be misled into thinking that a large heavy iron is better value. The iron's capacity for creating heat and moisture is the important factor.

Water for a steam iron

If you live in a hard-water area, do be careful about filling your steam iron straight from the tap. Use distilled water. This can be bought from most garages and pharmacists. But a good and cheap alternative is simply to collect the melted ice from around the freezing compartment of a refrigerator or freezer. This often contains little particles of dust and food and so it should be filtered through two thicknesses of muslin before use. It can be stored in a bottle or plastic container.

Correct Ironing Temperature

Symbol	max temp	for
*	120°C (248°F) – cool iron	acetete, acrylic, nylon
**	160°C (320°F) – warm iron	polyester/cotton mixtures, wool
***	210°C (410°F) – hot iron	·cotton, linen, viscose

Safety

Look at an electric blanket regularly for signs of damage: a check every month is necessary if the blanket is more than a year old. Look for scorch marks or fraying and check that flexes which may be concealed under the bed are not frayed.

Flex	The flex of your iron should be at least 7 ft 6 in (2.3 m) long so that you can iron comfortably at board level.
Storage	To store an electric blanket safely in summer spread it out flat on a spare bed if possible. If not then fold or roll it loosely and put it in a strong box. Make sure it is not crushed by other things on top of it and do not put it in a warm cupboard.
Washing	If you can wash your blanket then check its size with a tape measure before washing. Then afterwards you should gently pull and coax it back to the correct size. Dry it naturally without any kind of artificial heat. The best way is to hang it over the washing line in the shade.

Household emergencies

Power cuts	In case of power failure always make sure that you have the things you will need all together in a handy place. Put a few candles, a box of matches, your camping stove and perhaps a gas lantern all in a box or on the same shelf of a cupboard. Don't forget to keep holders for the candles, too, so that they will stand steady – a couple of old saucers in the box will do. Keep a torch in the box, and make sure the batteries are working.
Fuses	Keep several different sorts of fuses and wire by the fuse box and make sure that if you use them up they are replaced immediately. Also keep a small pocket torch by the fuse box.
The washing machine	If it stops working check first that the rubber hoses are not blocked.

Burning fat

Never throw water or any kind of liquid on to burning oil or fat. Either smother it with a damp cloth or towel, or if it is on the floor throw earth, sand or even flour over it.

Fires

Should a chimney catch alight, close all the doors and windows in the room tightly, throw a few handfuls of common salt on to the fire, fix a wet blanket in front of the grate to shut out any draught and call the fire brigade, if necessary.

If someone's clothing catches fire wrap a blanket, a carpet or something similar tightly round him, or roll him over and over on the floor in a blanket. Don't let him move about and especially not into the open air as this can fan the flames.

Scalds

If you burn your hand taking hot food from the oven, or scald yourself with boiling water, put your hand at once under cold water. This should help take away the pain and takes the heat from the tissues. Don't put any kind of grease or other cover on it.

Bleeding

The best way to stop bleeding from a cut or from the nose is to apply pressure to the spot, either with a pad, tying a bandage or scarf round, or pinching the nostrils together hard.

Stings

A paste of bicarbonate of soda and water applied to a sting will gradually take the pain away, but do be sure to remove the sting first with tweezers.

Water supply

Always know the whereabouts of the stopcock for the incoming water mains. In any kind of emergency such as a burst pipe turn it off straight away to minimize damage.

SECTION THREE
IN THE KITCHEN

Cookery terms

Au gratin	A dish which is covered in sauce, sprinkled with breadcrumbs and then dotted with fat and browned under the grill (broiler). Cheese is often mixed with the crumbs.
Compote	A stewed dish, usually of fruit.
Consommé	Soup made from clear meat stock.
Fricassée	A dish in which cooked meat is reheated in a sauce.
Jardinière	A garnish of several different vegetables arranged separately.
Lyonnaise	Cooked with onions.
Macédoine	A mixture of diced fruit or vegetables.
Marinade	A mixture of vinegar, oil and seasoning – or wine – in which food is soaked for several hours before cooking.
Mornay	With a cheese sauce.
Parboil	To boil for only part of the cooking time. The food is then cooked in some other way until ready.
Roux	A mixture of melted fat and flour which you then use to make flavoured sauces.
Sauté	Fried in shallow fat.
Sear	To brown the surface of meat by using a fierce heat for a short time.
Tepid	Just warm to the finger. A mixture of two parts of cold water and one part of boiling water gives about the right heat.
Vinaigrette	A mixture of oil, vinegar and seasonings usually served with a green salad.

Oven Temperature Chart:

	°F	°C	Gas Mark (UK only)
Very cool	225	110	¼
	250	130	½
Cool	275	140	1
	300	150	2
Moderate	325	160	3
	350	180	4
Moderately hot	375	190	5
	400	200	6
Hot	425	220	7
	450	230	8
Very hot	475	240	9
	500	250	10

Metric Conversion Chart:

Oz/fl. oz	Equivalent g/ml	Oz/fl. oz	Equivalent g/ml
1	28	6	170
2	57	7	198
3	85	8	226
4	113	9	255
5 (¼ pint)	142	10 (½ pint)	283

Temperature Conversions

To convert degrees Centigrade (Celsius) to the Fahrenheit equivalent use the following formula:

$(°C \times 1.8) + 32 = °F$ e.g. $(100 \times 1.8) + 32 = 212°F$
$100°C = 212°F$

To convert degrees Fahrenheit to the Centigrade equivalent:

$$\frac{(F - 32)}{1.8} = °C$$ e.g. $\frac{(212 - 32)}{1.8} = 100°C$

Vegetables

Pulses	Soak in cold water overnight, then boil and simmer until tender. Do not add salt until they are cooked: if you add it at the beginning they may stay slightly hard.
Boiling vegetables	Don't throw out the water in which you cook vegetables, but use it to add to soups and stocks. If you sauté vegetables in hot fat just before boiling, it will help seal in the nutrients otherwise lost in cooking. To keep that lovely bright green colour in vegetables when cooking them add a touch of bicarbonate of soda to the water.
To keep vegetables fresh	If cabbage or any other green vegetables are looking a little forlorn you can freshen them by dunking them in a bowl of cold water, giving them a good shake. Wrap them in a tea-towel and put them in the refrigerator for two hours. Always take vegetables out of plastic bags as they will very quickly go limp and then bad unless air circulates round them. If you are picking vegetables from your own garden for the freezer do try to pick them early in the day to get them at their freshest.
Blanching	If you do not have a blanching basket for vegetables, then tie about a pound of vegetables at a time in a muslin bag and plunge that into boiling water, making sure you have a string at the top to pull it out.
Cooking smells	To prevent unpleasant smells from cooking cabbage or other strong-smelling vegetables, put a small container of vinegar near the hob or oven.

Salads

To crisp up lettuce or watercress put it into a bowl of cold water for half an hour with a few slices of raw potato, or a spoonful of sugar. Or damp it slightly, wrap loosely in a tea-towel and put in the refrigerator for half an hour. Salad easily go limp, but if you put it in an airtight plastic bowl it will keep for at least two weeks in the refrigerator, even if you open it to take a few leaves out at intervals. It will stay far crisper than if kept in a plastic bag.

Young nasturtium leaves gathered from the garden are very good in salads and sandwiches. Wash the leaves well.

Brussels sprouts

Brussels sprouts often retain small pieces of grit and insects. To help draw these out cut a slot in the base of each sprout and put them in a bowl of salted water before cooking.

Carrots

To skin carrots easily rather than scraping them, drop them into boiling water for a few minutes as if blanching them. Take them out and put into cold water briefly before skinning them.

If you buy carrots with their tops on or pick them from the garden, take the tops off as quickly as possible to avoid loss of moisture and freshness.

Tomatoes

When baking tomatoes in the oven it is always a good idea to give them a little support to help them keep a good shape. Sit them in a foil cup.

If you cut tomatoes vertically instead of horizontally you will find you get firmer slices. If the tomatoes are going just a little soft then firm them up by placing in a bowl of iced water before cutting.

If you are using tomatoes in any cooked dish, such as a soup or stew, always skin them before cooking.

To skin tomatoes fill a bowl with boiling water and dip the tomatoes in. You will find the skin peels off very easily.

57

Mushrooms

To dry mushrooms, wipe with a dry cloth, cut away brown underneath part and then peel off the skin. Put in a cool oven on a baking sheet lined with paper and let them dry. Keep in paper bags in a dry place and when you want to use them put in cold water or gravy and they will almost regain their natural size. When cleaning mushrooms don't dip them right into water or soak them because they absorb water quickly and become soggy. Just wipe the surface gently, using the back of a clean scouring pad.

Onions

To keep an onion you have partly used, smear a little oil on to the cut side and then wrap tightly in foil. This will reduce the smell as much as possible.

It is the oil in the onion which causes eyes to water. To stop it, make sure that when you peel the onion you take out the fine film of skin which lies between the dry layers and the flesh as this contains the oil. Alternatively, pop the onion into the fridge or freezer before you cut it to stabilize the oils. Or peel under water.

Freezing onions

It is often worthwhile if you have a freezer to chop up 0.5 kg (1 lb) of onions finely all at once. If you do shed tears it will only be once instead of several times. Separate the onions into manageable portions of the size you are likely to use for various dishes and freeze them in empty yogurt pots, margarine containers or ice cream pots.

Cauliflower

To keep cauliflower fresh and white when freezing, add a teaspoonful of vinegar to the blanching water.

Turnips

The flavour of turnips and carrots is much improved if a pinch or two of sugar is added to the water when cooking.

Potatoes	To make old potatoes nice and floury, pour off the water they have been cooked in, then cover the pan with a clean cloth or a piece of greaseproof paper, replace the lid and let them steam for five minutes.
New potatoes	Always put new potatoes into water which is already boiling. Do not start them off in cold and bring them to the boil as with older potatoes. If you do not have as much time as you would like to make roast potatoes to go with a roast joint, then boil the potatoes first until they are more than half cooked before roasting them.
Frying and baking potatoes	When making chips you will get better results if you get all the starch out first. To do this simply prepare the chips in advance and then let them stand in cold water for ten minutes or so before using. You will see the water taking on a cloudy tinge as the starch goes into it. Drain the chips and cook as usual. Always rub the skin of potatoes with salt before baking.
Cucumber	A cut cucumber can be kept stalk downwards in cold water in much the same way as flowers. Cover the cut side with foil. Generally, though, cucumbers are better stored wrapped in brown paper in a cold pantry rather than in a refrigerator.
Casseroling vegetables	You can cook different kinds of vegetables in the same casserole as the meat: just wrap each variety in separate pieces of buttered foil, closing them tightly. The flavours will then be kept completely separate.
Dried vegetables	If you live in a hard-water area put a level teaspoon of bicarbonate of soda in the water when cooking dried vegetables, to make them tender.

59

Meat

Beef
It should be bright red, fine grained, firm and elastic to the touch with a marbling of fine cream fat. Prime cuts should contain very little gristle.

Lamb
It should be a light pink if young and darker if older. The fat should be white and the bones moist and red at the joints.

Mutton
It should be bright red with yellow fat.

Pork
It should be pink and the fat should be firm and white. The flesh should be finely grained and smooth.

Carving
Meat must always be carved across the grain and not with it.

Leftovers
Use up leftover meat by mincing it together with vegetables. Add mayonnaise and seasoning and you have a tasty sandwich spread.
Don't waste leftover sausagemeat. Mix it with leftover mashed potato and fry.

Extra flavourings
Add half a bottle of stout to a stew for a special occasion to give extra richness. When making gravy for a roast, strain off the fat and instead of adding gravy browning or cornflour, pour half a glass of wine round the roasting pan, mixing with the juices. Cook gently for two minutes before serving as gravy. For a duck you can add orange juice and redcurrant jelly to the juices.

Cooking ham and bacon
When frying or grilling ham or bacon, make small cuts on the edges to prevent it curling during cooking.

Salted meat or fish
Soak a bacon joint, or any salty meat or fish, in water before cooking to take away some of the surplus salt.

Fish

Curing

This method of home curing is good for herring, mackerel and other small types of fish. Choose perfectly fresh fish, gut, scale and clean but don't wash. With salt and water make a brine strong enough to float an egg, and put in the fish, covering completely. Leave for 18 hours. When ready, drain, place in layers in an earthenware vessel, covering each layer thickly with salt. Cover closely to exclude air and store in a cool dry place. The fish must be soaked well before cooking.

Soaking

Freshwater fish will be improved by soaking for two hours (after cleaning) in well-salted water to which two tablespoons of vinegar have been added.

Cooking fish in milk

If you poach fish and want it to retain its white appearance add 5 cm (2") of lemon peel to the milk.
If you bake any white fish in enough milk to cover it, you will have a ready-made parsley sauce. Just add finely chopped parsley to the liquor when the fish is done and some thickening.

Mussels

When cooking mussels, wash them and remove all grit and their 'beards'. You may need to use wire wool.

Baking

Cake mixtures If you are making a cake when the doorbell rings, you may well forget which ingredients have been added and which not. So it is a good idea always to put the ingredients required for the recipe on one side of the bowl, and then as you add them transfer to the other side of the bowl. If you follow the same simple routine every time you will not get confused if interrupted.

Dried fruit To prevent glacé cherries sinking in a fruit cake, wash off the excess syrup and dry well before using. Dried fruit and dates can be coated with a little flour before using in cakes to prevent them all sinking to the bottom.
To give cakes an extra flavour soak the dried fruit overnight in a little sherry.

Dried milk Use dried milk for baking occasionally as it can be cheaper than fresh.

Flour It is cheaper to buy self-raising flour rather than plain flour and baking powder as well.
You can make an extra-fine flour for special cakes by substituting some cornflour for flour.

Tin (Pan) Sizes

If you want to substitute round for square tins (pans) use this chart to work out the equivalent size in pint capacity.

Round Tin (Pan)	Litres/Pints	Square Tin (Pan)
18 cm/7 inches	1/2	12.5 cm/5 inches
21 cm/8 inches	1.5/3	18 cm/7 inches
23 cm/9 inches	2.25/4	21 cm/8 inches
25 cm/10 inches	3.5/6	23 cm/9 inches
28 cm/11 inches	4.5/8	25 cm/10 inches
30 cm/12 inches	5.5/10	28 cm/11 inches
35 cm/14 inches	7/12	30 cm/12 inches

Baking tins and linings

Although shining new baking tins may look splendid they will not give the best results as food does not brown well in them. So bake any new ones in a hot oven to dull them down before actually using for food. If your baking tins are not non-stick and you use greaseproof paper for lining then cut out several linings to fit the tins you use most often and keep them in a kitchen drawer. When putting a piece of wax paper into the sides of a cake tin, cut a strip about 1.25 cm (½″) wider than required, then bend up 1.25 cm (½″) along one side of the strip and with scissors snip at regular intervals all the way along. Put the nicked edges into the bottom of the round tin and it will fit nicely.

Is the cake cooked?

A small cake in the oven will normally show signs of shrinking away from the side of the pan when it is cooked. To test whether a cake is cooked push a warmed skewer or knife right into the centre. If it comes out clean the cake is cooked, if the mixture still adheres to it then the cake needs a little longer. If a cake has a cracked top, rises unevenly or is a dark rather than a golden brown, the oven may be too hot. If the crust is unduly thick, the cake dry and the texture coarse, then the oven is not hot enough.

Choux pastry

To ensure éclairs or anything made of choux pastry rises well place a baking pan or roasting pan filled with water in the bottom of the oven. The gently rising steam will do the trick.

Yeast

Do you use fresh or dried yeast? Remember that 14 g (½ oz) of dried yeast equals 28 g (1 oz) fresh yeast. Fresh yeast will keep in the fridge for up to a month if it is tied loosely in a plastic bag. It will keep in the freezer for up to a year if it is wrapped really tightly.

63

Sugar

To ensure a constant supply of vanilla-flavoured sugar required in some recipes put some sugar in a screw-top jar and put a vanilla pod in with it.
If you run out of caster sugar for a recipe then put the required weight of granulated sugar into your coffee grinder and grind until fine.

Pastry making

When you are rolling out pastry remember that if you are either right- or left-handed you will tend to exert more pressure on that side, so do try to put equal pressure on it.
To prevent flan pastry going soggy you can brush some egg white over the surface. Also put a baking sheet in the pre-set oven and put the pie plate on top of the hot sheet to give extra heat to the bottom layer of pastry.
If you run out of ingredients to make pastry for puddings then use biscuits instead. Crush 112 g (4 oz) digestive biscuits by putting them in a plastic bag and then banging them inside the bag with a rolling pin. Melt 56 g (2 oz) margarine, stir in the biscuits and a little sugar and press the mixture into a 18 cm (7") sandwich tin, bringing it well up the sides. Leave to set and then add any filling.

Eggs

Crack The Egg Code

In the member countries of the EEC all eggs have a code on the box which gives various details. The first number gives the week in which it was packed. This runs from the first week to the last week in the year, i.e. the first week in January is week 1. The next series of numbers give the country, the area and the packing station of the eggs. The United Kingdom number is 9 and each area has a special code number, as does each packing station. Therefore, if a box is coded 3 9/7/888 you will know it was packed in the third week of January in station no. 888 in the area of Britain indicated.

Sizing

In the EEC, eggs are sized as follows:

Size 1=70g (2½ oz)   **Size 4**=55g (2 oz)

Size 2=65g (2¼ oz)   **Size 5**=50g (1½ oz)

Size 3=60g (2 oz)   **Size 6**=45g (1½ oz)

Boiling

If you boil eggs straight from the refrigerator they are likely to crack. If you have forgotten to take them out in advance hold them under the hot tap for a few minutes before putting into the water to boil. They should then remain whole.

Freshness

You can test an egg for freshness by putting it in a bowl of water. If it settles towards the bottom the egg is fresh, if it goes to the top it is not.

Frying

Eggs will not stick or break in the frying pan if you add a teaspoon of flour to the hot fat before cracking the shells and putting in the eggs.

65

Poaching

If you don't have a proper poacher and your eggs tend to spread all over the pan, lightly grease small flan rings or (if you want fancy shapes) metal biscuit-cutters and break the eggs into these. To get really nicely rounded poached eggs try this method. Before you poach the eggs, dip each one in its shell into boiling water while you count up to thirty, then take it out, break it into the pan and poach in the usual way.

Salt

Salt has to be carefully used when cooking eggs since it breaks down the white and tends to make it watery. So don't add salt to the water in which you poach an egg as it will cause the white to detach itself in strings from the yolk. The correct thing to add to the water is vinegar, which has the effect of sealing the egg white.

Whisking egg whites

When separating egg whites for beating make sure you do not get any yolk in with the white or it will not beat firmly. If you do drop any in, the best way to remove it is to use part of the empty egg shell to lift it out.

If you use an electric beater start beating slowly and gradually increase the speed. If you overbeat you will get a grainy texture and it will separate into dry and lumpy particles. Add a pinch of salt towards the end of the beating.

If you intend to beat egg whites for meringues or other recipes, you must store them at room temperature for several hours beforehand. If whites are too cold they will not whisk as stiffly as they should.

Leftovers

To keep leftover egg yolks in good condition add a pinch of salt to them and store in a small covered container for up to two days. Egg whites will keep for up to two weeks in a covered jar in the refrigerator.

Economy   Don't ever pay more for brown eggs
                   than for white – they have no more
                   food value.

Duck eggs   Duck eggs when used for baking will
                   each be the equivalent of one-and-a-half
                   hen's eggs.
                   When using duck eggs care must be
                   taken to cook them thoroughly as they
                   are more likely to carry harmful bacteria
                   than hen's eggs. So don't poach them.

Sauces   When adding eggs to a hot sauce or
                   milk for custard you must be careful to
                   see that the sauce or milk is below
                   boiling point, or the eggs will set in small
                   lumps and curdle the mixture. A sauce
                   should not be allowed to boil after the
                   eggs have been added; just heat it
                   gently.

Storage   Eggs should be stored well away from
                   any foods with a strong odour, because
                   the shells are porous and allow odours
                   to pass through.

Freezing   You can freeze eggs (so you can always
                   be sure of having some for baking if you
                   run out of fresh ones). Don't freeze
                   them in their shells – break them and
                   whisk lightly. Freeze the yolks and
                   whites separately. The yolks should be
                   mixed with a little salt or sugar.

Bread

Proving

Brown bread does not need to rise twice as most recipes suggest. Simply make in the usual way and knead for ten minutes. Place it straight into the greased pans, leave until it doubles in size and then put in the oven. The texture will be excellent without a double rising. If your dough does not seem to be rising as fast as it should, sit the pans on top of the cooker and turn on the oven (which should be preheated for the bread anyway). The gentle heat reaches through the top of the oven and to the bottom of the tins, helping the dough to rise.

Texture

To improve the texture of a brown loaf use half brown and half white flour rather than all brown.

Stale bread

If bread has become slightly stale then dampen it slightly and put it in a warm to hot oven where it will soon freshen. This applies to rolls as well as loaves.

To vary the crust

For a crisp crust on home-made bread leave the loaves as they are when they go into the oven, but for a softer crust rub with buttered paper and then when they come out of the oven, cover with a cloth for five to ten minutes. For an attractive top to brown bread sprinkle the top with some wholemeal flour, bran or cracked wheat before baking.

Baking

To ascertain whether or not your bread is ready turn the loaf out of the tin and tap it on the bottom. If it has a hollow sound, it is ready.

Cutting bread

Fresh bread can be tricky and it often crumbles away. To avoid this, heat a thin-bladed knife in hot water for a few minutes, dry it and then slice.

Dairy products

Custard   If a baked custard becomes watery it is usually caused by mixing the eggs with cold milk. Warm the milk first and this will not happen.

Butter   Make 0.5 kg (1 lb) of butter stretch by bringing it to room temperature. Then beat it to a cream with an egg beater and add two cups of milk a little at a time. Beat until all the milk is absorbed then chill until solid again.

Sour milk   If a recipe calls for only a small amount of sour milk you can make your own by adding one tablespoon of vinegar to the milk and stirring. You can add the same to cream to make sour cream.

Milk puddings   For children who are difficult about taking cooked milk puddings you can disguise the milkiness with a little added colouring.

Meringues   To prevent meringues sticking during cooking, thoroughly butter the baking sheets, let the butter cool completely and then sprinkle the sheet evenly with some flour. Never add the flour while the butter is liquid.

Batter   To make a really crisp batter for fish and fritters do not use egg in it, but instead use self-raising flour and water with seasoning.
It is a good idea to put any kind of batter you are using for pancakes into a jug rather than a bowl. It is easier to pour out just the right amount.

Milk   If you have no refrigerator, keep milk fresh in summer by standing it in cold water with a piece of clean, damp muslin over the top of the jug with the ends of the material in the water.

Catering for large numbers

Bread	Large white loaves, thinly sliced, will usually cut into about 22 slices. One large loaf will need 225 g (½ lb) of butter to make sandwiches.
Tea	For a large number of people, remember that 60-80 g (2-3 oz) tea is sufficient for 4.5 litres (½ gallon) of boiling water to give a medium strength drink. It will make about 36 cups and will need 1 litre (2 pints) milk.
Sandwiches	Sandwiches will keep well overnight if packed in plastic bags or stacked on a large tray and covered completely with a damp cloth. If putting a large number of sandwiches on a table try to keep them covered with a damp cloth as long as possible to keep them fresh.
Ice cream	A gallon of ice cream (4½ litres) served with fruit salad will serve about 35 people.
Extra trays	If you run out of trays cover breadboards with some tin foil or use thick cardboard covered with foil or with adhesive plastic material.

Coffee

To test for chicory

To test whether ground coffee is pure coffee or has chicory added to it, throw a small teaspoonful of the grounds on to the surface of some water in a tumbler or a cup. If the coffee is pure it will float, but if there is chicory present it will sink rapidly and stain the water.

Roasting

If you can mange to get your own coffee berries you can roast your own coffee. Simply put the berries in a clean pan and put it over a gas or electric ring. Constant even heat is required and stirring, shaking and revolving of the berries is necessary to get an even nut-brown colour. You can then add a tiny quantity of fresh butter or caster sugar, just enough to give the berries a gloss. It's important that the berries are not blackened or the coffee will have a bitter taste. Roast only enough for two or three days' supply at a time.

Percolated coffee

Put a tiny pinch of salt with your ground coffee in the percolator and you will find the flavour improves.

Nuts

Almonds and pistachios

To peel them cover the nuts with boiling water, let them stay there for about five minutes, strain and replace them in the basin, covering with cold water. When cool, drain and remove the skins by pressing each nut between the thumb and forefinger.

Storage

Because of their oil content, nuts easily turn rancid so they should always be stored in an airtight container and preferably at a low temperature. They keep much better in their shells.

71

Chestnuts   To skin chestnuts, pierce the shell of each nut with a pointed knife before blanching in boiling water and cooking for one or two minutes. Leave the nuts in hot water before peeling, and reheat them if they become hard to peel as they cool. Use a small knife to cut away the shell and the skin at the same time.

Hazelnuts   For hazelnuts, bake in the oven at 180°C (350°F, Gas mark 4) until they are golden brown – the skins will crack and start to peel. Let the nuts cool slightly then rub off the skins with a coarse cloth.

Miscellaneous tips

Cornflakes   If kept in a packet too long cornflakes lose their crispness – the same applies to potato crisps. Both will crisp again if you put them in the oven for a short time, but do not let them burn.

Olive oil   Always choose the best possible kind of olive oil. The best qualify is a light green, but any which is almost colourless shading to a golden yellow may be safely used. Avoid a deep brownish yellow or dark green oil.

Candied peel   To make your own, take the rinds off sound young fruits, cut into pieces, take away any pulp and boil in water till soft. Put into strong cold syrup and leave until the peel becomes semi-transparent, then dry slowly.

Rhubarb   Improve the flavour of stewed rhubarb by adding 2 tablespoons of syrup during cooking. You can also improve the colour with a piece of red table jelly. To reduce the amount of sugar needed to sweeten acid fruit such as rhubarb, add a pinch of bicarbonate of soda to the fruit in the pan.

Caramel

To make liquid caramel put 225 g (1 lb) caster (confectioners') sugar and a tablespoon of water into a pan and heat until dark brown. Boil, add water to the sugar to make ½ litre (1 pint), stir until it boils and simmer until the caramel acquires the consistency of syrup. This should make about ½ litre (1 pint). Leave until cold and bottle it until required. Leave in a cool, dark place.

Fats and oils

Fats and oils should be kept away from foods which have a strong flavour as they can easily be tainted.
If you want to use oil for mixing cakes and pastries, then use only 28 g (1 oz) for every 56 g (2 ozs) of whatever fat the recipe calls for.
Hard dripping and cooking fats are very much improved if they are beaten with a fork to soften and 2 teaspoons of oil are added to each 112 g (4 oz) of fat and then beaten in thoroughly.
To clean sediment from oil or liquid fat, add potato slices and fry until they are brown.

Spices

Only keep a small amount of spices and flavourings in the kitchen and do not be tempted to buy racks containing several bottles you will never use. They become stale and lose flavour in a fairly short time. Store those you have in an airtight jar and try to keep them away from direct light.

Cheese

Keep any chunks of stale cheese and grind them up with raw onion to make a tasty spread.
A little mustard added to cheese dishes helps to bring out the flavour.
A supply of ready-grated cheese for soups, sandwiches and garnishes can be stored in a covered jar and will keep quite well in a refrigerator for some weeks. This is a good way of using up small pieces.

73

Stewed fruit

Less sugar is needed if you let the fruit boil for about ten minutes before adding the sugar.

Mayonnaise

When making a mayonnaise you must add the oil drop by drop to prevent curdling. If the mixture ceases to be smooth then put another egg yolk into a clean bowl and add the mixture to that bowl very slowly, and that should get the smoothness back.

Salad dressing

To make a quick salad dressing from yogurt, just blend a pot of natural yogurt with a little lemon juice and seasoning and toss the salad in it.

Celery flakes

Keep celery leaves and dry them by cooking in a very slow oven. Then rub them through your fingers or use a sieve and the resulting flakes can be used to flavour all kinds of savoury dishes.

Cucumber

When making cucumber sandwiches put the salt on the bread and butter, not on the cucumber. This will make it more easily digestible. And if you cover cucumber with salt for an hour and then pour off the liquid drawn out, you will also find it easier to digest.

Fruit

When peeling oranges for a fruit salad first soak in boiling water for five minutes or so. The white pithy part will peel off quite easily and leave the oranges clean and ready for slicing. And if you have any orange pulp to spare, save it and add it next time you are stewing apples to give a new flavour.

To prevent apples discolouring when peeling, use a silver knife and put them in salted water if not being used immediately.

To prevent peeled bananas going brown, cover with lemon juice. Do not store bananas in the refrigerator as they will go black even in their skins.

Pasta

Pasta should be a rich golden colour when raw and should be cooked just long enough to be firm but not tough, tender but not slimy.

Stuffings

If you want to use stale bread for stuffings (and fresh is best), soak it in water first and then squeeze out the excess moisture. It can be heated in the oven or a pan for a few minutes to help it to dry out.

If you cook your stuffing for a savoury dish separately it will be much firmer in texture than if it is cooked as part of the dish.

Herbs

To dry herbs in the kitchen, gather them just before they begin to flower, dry them indoors, then strip the leaves from the stalks, put them in a moderately hot oven on baking tins until crisp then rub them between the palms of the hands. Pass through a sieve to remove the small stalks and then put into hot dry bottles, cork and store.

Salt

Two or three grains of rice in the salt cellar will absorb any dampness and prevent the salt from sticking when using the cellar.

Jam

To remove the scum from the surface of jam drop in a knob of butter just before the jam is removed from the heat. This gives a shine and causes the scum to disappear.

When making jam always cook fruit thoroughly *before* adding the sugar so that you release the pectin and can be sure of getting a good set. Do not let it come to the boil until all the sugar is added.

If you are making jam with some kind of large berry such as strawberry then leave the jam to cool for a little before putting into jars. This helps to keep the fruit suspended evenly instead of it rising to the top.

It can be useful to have some pectin stock available if you are making jam from fruits which lack this and will not set well. To make this stock use apple scraps (cores, peel, etc). Simmer ½ kg (1 lb) apple scraps in 0.25 litre (½ pint) water until the apples are pulpy. Strain through a jelly bag and then put the juice back in the pan and bring to the boil. Put into pre-heated jars and cover if you want to use soon. If you want to keep it put it in Kilner jars.

When making marrow jam a piece of citron peel added gives a delicious flavour.

Bran

If your family won't take bran but you'd like to increase the fibre in their diet then sprinkle some bran on top of soups . . . and also add some to bread and scones when you bake them.

Skimming fat

To remove fat from stocks and stews while still warm, first skim off as far as possible with a metal spoon and then tear a piece of absorbent tissue paper from the kitchen roll, use it in wide strips and draw the strips across the surface of the liquid, absorbing as much fat as possible with the paper.

Breadcrumbs

Don't throw away stale bread. Remove crusts, cut into strips and bake in a low oven for 15-20 minutes until golden brown. Serve with soup. Alternatively dry the crusts out thoroughly in a low oven, put into a plastic bag and crush into crumbs with a rolling pin. Keep them in an airtight jar for use as a coating for fish, chicken, etc.

Jam fritters

To make an inexpensive pudding, cut some thin slices of bread, taking off the crusts. Spread thinly with butter or margarine and jam and put together to make a sandwich. Cut each one into four and then fry in a little hot oil until golden on both sides. You can also deep-fry them. These jam fritters are delicious served with custard.

Allergies

Some people are allergic to vinegar and for anyone who is, then the substitution of lemon juice in most recipes will work out perfectly well.

Food for babies

Proprietary baby foods can be expensive but there is no reason why ordinary family foods cannot be used for the baby. Start off by sieving things like vegetables, potato and gravy, stewed fruits and then gradually introduce finely minced meat and fish.

77

Cooker craft

Rings

Try always to use a saucepan on the correct ring for the saucepan's size, so that the ring itself is completely covered. This saves the ring from warping. Do not have the rings switched on unless they are being used and have something to cover them. Choose good quality pans with flat bases which will make good contact with the heat and result in greater efficiency and a good saving of fuel.

The grill

Always heat the grill (broiler) before you use it, rather than putting the food underneath and then switching on. Try to avoid piercing the food as you turn it – if possible use tongs to do this.

To avoid constantly cleaning out your grill (broiler) pan, especially if you are grilling fatty foods, then line the base of the pan with a piece of foil. It can be taken out and either thrown away or washed for reuse in hot soapy water. This will avoid a build up of grease on your pan.

Do not put dishes too close to each other in the oven or the circulation of hot air will be stopped and the baking may well be uneven. Most ovens need about 2-3 inches of space between the sides of the oven and the dishes of food.

Cleaning the cooker

If you do spill any grease, fat or food on your stove wipe up the spills straight away, because the heat makes them harden very quickly indeed, and harder to remove.

Proprietary oven cleaners are expensive. Next time you clean the oven, make up a paste of bicarbonate of soda and water and spread it over the cleaned surface. You will find that the next time you spill something it will rub off easily with a damp cloth.

Equipment techniques

To sharpen scissors

A do-it-yourself method is to take an empty milk bottle and to try to cut the top off it. You will not succeed, of course, but you will find the scissors become sharper after a few attempts.

To sharpen knives

If using a steel to sharpen carbon steel carving knives hold the steel slanting upwards in your left hand, and, holding the knife in your right hand, draw it rapidly up and down the steel with the knife slanting very slightly inwards. Avoid having too acute an angle or the cutting edge of the knife will have too direct a contact with the steel.

Burnt saucepans

Fill the pan with salt and water and let it stand for 24 hours, then bring the water to the boil. The burnt particles should then come off easily.

Dishwashers

If you have any hand-painted bone china be very careful about putting it in the dishwasher for the pattern may disappear. Do not put in anything made of wood, or with glue on the handle, or which has worn silver plate, as damage may be caused.

Replanning a kitchen

Draw out on squared paper a plan of the area and scale down the appliances you have, using an accurate comparative scale. Cut out the appliance shapes and then simply move them around the squared paper plan till you get an arrangement which suits you.

Frying pans

To season new enamel frying pans so that food does not stick, spread some dry salt all over the surface of the pan, rub it in then wipe it off. Then heat some oil in the pan to smoking point for a few minutes, making sure it covers the whole surface, then pour away.

Opening bottles	If you find it impossible to open a screw-top bottle, put on a rubber glove. You will find this gives an excellent grip.
Casseroles	The first time you use a new earthenware casserole which can be used on top of the cooker, it is advisable to fill it with cold water to which a little salt and vinegar has been added, then place it over heat and bring slowly to the boil. This process should be repeated in a slow oven. Never take a hot casserole and fill it with cold water or stand it on a cold surface, as this will make it liable to crack.
Dispersing smells	A cloth wrung out in vinegar and swung through the air will get rid of any musty or household smells in a room. To keep a refrigerator smelling sweet use half a teaspoon of bicarbonate of soda in a bowl of water for washing the interior. The same solution put into a Thermos flask will take away any odours.
Measuring quantities	To measure a level spoon or cup of dry ingredients run the blade of a knife across the top of the spoon or cup. To weigh anything which is slightly sticky always dust a little flour on to the scale pan first. Inaccurate weighing of syrup and treacle can often cause recipes to go wrong. So to be absolutely sure you have got it right weigh the tin of syrup, take some out and weigh the tin again.
Replenishing stocks	Keep a pad and pencil handy in the kitchen ready to make a note of anything as soon as you run out of it or are nearly out of it. Then you will remember to add it to the list for your next shopping trip.
Glass utensils	If food should stick to the sides of either a glass dish or a glass saucepan, then fill it with water and leave it to soak away.

Cans	If you spot any cans in your cupboard which have 'blown' – that is, bulge at the top and bottom – do not use them as this indicates the food inside is bad.
Jelly moulds	If a jelly or cold sweet seems to be sticking in the mould, run a knife round the rim and dip the mould into hot water. It should then slide out easily.
Salad bowls	If a wooden salad bowl needs a bit of renovation try using the very finest grade of steel wool to remove stains.

Freezer terms

Dry pack	Freeze the food just as it is without adding any extra liquid or sugar.
Open freeze	Do not pack the items together, but spread them out on some sort of tray and allow to freeze individually. When frozen put them together in a container. This is useful for rosettes of cream or potatoes or anything easily damaged.
Syrup pack	Pack fresh fruits in cartons and fill up with a syrup of sugar and water.
Headspace	There must be a space left between any food and the top of its container. Often foods will expand as they cool and if packed too tightly will tend to force the lid off.
Temperature gradient	This is where there is a different temperature in different parts of the freezer. It can cause any foods which have not been adequately packaged to dry out.
Burn	If foods are not packed in containers or heavy plastic which will give them sufficient protection they can 'burn' or lose moisture to an extent where they are too dry to eat or to have any taste.

81

Freezer tips

Ice cubes

To give a party look to drinks, make the ice cubes in your freezer with food colouring added to the water or put a small curl of lemon peel or even an olive into each section of the tray before freezing.

If you need to make several trays of ice cubes and store them in a plastic bag, you may find they stick together. To prevent this, simply squirt them with soda – this should do the trick and they will easily separate.

Parsley

This is a very good thing to freeze, because when you take it out it will crumble beautifully between your fingers, saving the bother of chopping it. Freeze stalks too as they are flavourful and nourishing.

Roses

If you would like to have a rosebud from your garden on the Christmas table then try freezing one for it. Pick a bud which is not open but not too tight and put it in a plastic container. Fill with an inch of water, freeze and then top this up with more water. Leave in the freezer till required. The rose will only last a day or two when thawed out.

You can freeze full-blown rose heads in a container of water – then sit them in finger bowls as a decoration at a dinner party. As they thaw out the leaves will fall and gently scent the water for finger dipping.

Advance testing

If you are planning to freeze several dishes for a special dinner party you may like to make sure the mixture is exactly right. Freeze a tiny portion of each dish separately, and then a few days before the dinner you can take these out and do an advance test for taste and texture.

82

Moving house

Your freezer and the food in it can go with you on the removal van. Make sure it goes into the van last and then is out first and plugged in at your destination. For at least 24 hours before you move, put the freezer on fast freeze to make sure everything is really solid. If it is very full and too heavy to move, the food can be taken out, wrapped in newspaper and put back once the freezer itself has been loaded. At the other end the same procedure will have to be gone through.

Food in a freezer will normally stay frozen for up to 36 hours and certainly for 24. So in the event of a power failure cover the freezer with blankets or rugs to provide extra insulation and do not open the lid or door.

Containers

Keep old yogurt pots, cottage cheese and even margarine containers. They are very useful for freezing small quantities of food and can be used several times.

Carrots

Do not freeze carrots without blanching them, whatever the recipe books say, as they will emerge soggy and tasteless. Always blanch them no matter how young.

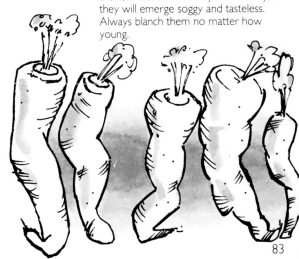

Repairs

If the freezer stops working, don't panic. Check the wiring, plug, socket and fuse before telephoning the repair man. If you have get expert help then do not open the freezer door if at all possible.

Fruit-juice cubes

If some of your family or friends drink spirits with orange as an addition you might like to freeze cubes of orange juice instead of water in an ice tray. They can be used too to give added coolness to summer soft drinks. Tomato juice and other fruit juice can be treated in the same way.

Electricity

Any insurance company will tell you that they get claims for lost food when someone accidentally switches off the freezer. So to prevent that, cover the switch at the socket outlet with a piece of adhesive tape. Remember NOT to switch the mains electricity off when you go on holiday or the freezer will be off too. If possible get the freezer put on a separate circuit so that everything else can be switched off at the main switch.

Tomato juice

To freeze tomato juice in a handy fashion pour it into an ice cube tray. When it has frozen, take out the blocks and store in a plastic bag for use as you need them. You can also freeze leftover gravy in this way and it can be easily popped into a stew.

Removing air from pack

When freezing, make sure all air is excluded, as it can cause discoloration and slow down the freezing process. How do you get all the air out of your packs? Simple – use a straw. Fix a twist tie loosely round the neck of the bag, put in the straw, suck out the air and then tighten the twist. Another alternative is to plunge the bag up to its neck in a bowl of cold water, forcing out the surplus air. Hold the neck of the bag above water, fix a twist tie, tighten it and lift the bag out of the water. Be sure to dry the outside of the bag before freezing.

Contamination

Cross-contamination of other foods in the freezer by fishy smells or flavours can be avoided by taking extra care in packing and if possible, by enclosing all your fish packs in a large plastic container or a very thick plastic bag.

Colour coding

You will find things more easily in the freezer if you try to colour code the various categories of food: blue for vegetables, yellow for fruit, red for meat and so on.

Scraping

Most chest freezers come supplied with a plastic spatula for scraping the frost from the sides. If you scrape away the excess regularly, about once a month, you will not need to have an annual defrosting session which means running down your stock of food.
If you do have to give your freezer an annual defrost then you can speed things up quite safely by placing a bowl of hot water in the bottom of the freezer once it is empty, or you can give a quick blow with your hair dryer. When defrosted give the interior a wipe over with a solution of bicarbonate of soda (one tablespoon to 1 litre (2 pints) of warm water) to keep it fresh.

Care of the freezer	To protect the outside of your freezer from any possible rusting (if you have it in a shed or garage) and to keep it looking fresh, polish the surface occasionally with either white furniture cream or car polish.
Fruit	If you have loads of fruit in your garden or friends have given you some and you cannot spare the time to make it into jam just freeze the fruit. Also buy Seville oranges in season and freeze them whole until you are ready to make them into marmalade. Citrus fruit freeze beautifully whole and without any packaging.
Choosing a freezer	If you are not very tall do think twice about buying a chest freezer as it can be tricky reaching right to the bottom of some of the larger versions.
Heat-sealing	If you do not have a machine for sealing the edges of plastic bags for freezer items you can heat-seal bags by using the edge of an electric iron at its coolest setting. Put the two edges of the bag together and protect the plastic from direct heat with two pieces of tissue paper. Make the seal near the top of the bag so that it can be cut off with the minimum of waste and the bag used again.
Drinks	Never put carbonated (fizzy) drinks in the freezer as there is the possibility of the low temperature causing a minor explosion.
Lemons	If you freeze lemons you will find that they grate like a dream and that the oil from the skin which is full of flavour does not escape.
Defrosting	If you want to defrost frozen food packs in a hurry, then hold them under cold running water.

SECTION FOUR
CARS & GARDENS

Pests

Aerosol sprays

Aerosol sprays to kill flies in the house are both popular and effective, but remember that they contain chemicals. Not all labels spell out the precautions you should take. So keep food covered when you are using these insect sprays, do not inhale the mist and keep it well away from pets and children. Remove any birds in cages from a room before spraying. If possible avoid direct contact with the chemical by using rubber gloves, and always wash your hands after using a spray.

Fleas

Cat fleas are quite common and they can be brought into the home quite easily. To avoid this risk make sure your cat wears an anti-flea collar.

Mice

To avoid mice coming into the house, check for any small holes there may be around skirting where cables, ducts or pipes go through the wall.
The best way to get rid of mice is to use a good old-fashioned trap. But forget all you've heard about using cheese as a bait. Tests show that mice prefer chocolate, dried fruit, nuts or lard.

Wasps

If you get a wasps' nest in the bricks or the attic don't attempt to deal with it yourself but call in the local authority or a pest-removal firm.

Flowers and foliage

Keeping flowers fresh

To keep cut flowers fresh for as long as possible cut off a small piece of the stem every day. If the stalks are woody the ends should be split for half an inch before putting into water, or crushed with a hammer. A little soda or salt added to the water will also help.

Poppies

The ends of the stems of poppies should be closed by dipping them into melted wax or burning them.

Irises

Cut the stems of iris in a slant and give them a deep drink of water before arranging them in a vase.

Lupins

To make lupins last longer first plunge their stems into boiling water and then put them in a bucket of cold water for a few hours. If you put a little starch into the water this will prevent the flowers dropping off quite so quickly.

Peonies

Peony stems should be cut off by half an inch and given a soak in warm water before arranging.

Woody shrubs

With rhododendron and any similar woody shrub such as azalea, hammer the ends of the stems well and put into hot water for a couple of hours before transferring to a vase.

Tulips

Wrap tulips in newspaper and leave them in warm water for a few hours before arranging. If you prick through the stem just under the head with a pin it makes them last longer.

Travelling with flowers

When travelling with flowers wrap them in several sheets of wet newspapers or a wad of damp cottonwool, then cover them with a plastic bag to retain the moisture.

89

Hydrangeas and hyacinths	These will benefit from a soaking in warm water before being put in a vase. Always crush the cut end of the stem.
Falling pollen	Any flowers which have pollen or leaves prone to falling off on to furniture can be treated with a squirt of hair lacquer to help prevent this.
Care of pot plants	If you have to go away and can't find a neighbour to look after your potted plants then try this method. Place alongside the pot a small bowl of water. Take a small piece of absorbent material and put one end of it into the bowl and the other into the plant pot. The plant will draw up water from the bowl through the material. Indoor plants can get very dusty and dull – so go over the leaves with a soft brush. If the leaves are not too small to handle, give the plant a gentle wash with mild suds. Large shiny-leaved plants can be finished off by polishing with a soft cloth.
Care of dried flowers	If you mix dried flowers or foliage with fresh ones from the garden to make an arrangement, paint the bottoms of the preserved items with nail varnish to keep them waterproof. Gourds, seed heads and berried branches which have been dried can be given a coat of clear varnish to help preserve them.
Table decorations	Make a colourful table decoration when fresh flowers aren't available or are too expensive, using rhododendron leaves. Pick some clusters from a shrub (there are usually about six leaves growing out of a centre containing next year's bud). Dip the stems in hot wax to keep the foliage fresh, then, using household or poster paint, paint the leaves red and the bud in the centre yellow. You then have an approximation to a poinsettia.

To dry flowers and foliage

Easily dried flowers like helichrysums, gypsophila and the globe thistle can be dried by hanging, heads down in a dark, dry, warm place, taking care not to bunch the flowers too closely together. An airing cupboard is ideal.

To dry plants which are fairly delicate, use the borax method. It can be used for both foliage and flowers. Put a layer of borax powder in an airtight box, place the plants on it and sprinkle some more powder until they are quite covered. Shut the lid and leave the box sealed for about a month. By that time they should have dried out completely. Prepare leaves for winter decorations by picking branches or twigs of leaves such as beech when they are at their best – in late spring or early summer. Split the ends of the stems, crush them and stand them in a container of water to which you have added a cupful of glycerine. They are ready when the leaves absorb the glycerine and slowly turn to bronze.

In the garden

Ponds and pools	Put a net over any ponds in autumn to catch all the falling leaves. A plastic ball floating on a garden pond in winter will prevent the surface freezing solid.
Sandpits	A children's sandpit should be in full view of one of the windows. It should not however be placed in full sunlight as children quickly become tired and hot.
Plant containers	An old sink makes a good plant trough. Stand it on a base of bricks, fill it with soil and plant what you like. Don't overcrowd it with plants but try to get a pleasing display of different heights.
Fencing	If you have natural wood fencing of any kind give it a protective coating of creosote every year to preserve the wood. But remember that creosote kills plants, so take care when applying it.
Spraying	Never attempt to use any garden sprays in a high wind, as it may blow chemicals into your neighbour's garden.
Bulbs	Be careful about buying bulbs in large quantities which appear to be cheap. These are often undersized bulbs which will not flower for a year or two or will only produce very small flowers. To have bulbs flowering in pots indoors in the spring you need to start them off in early October. Water freely and keep in a cool, dark place until the first shoots appear, then gradually increase the amount of light.
Planting vegetables	If you have a freezer check before you plant any particular variety of vegetables that it is suitable for freezing – it will usually indicate this on the back of the seed packet.

Potatoes

When planting seed potatoes, you will get better value for money by cutting them in half. As long as both halves have strong shoots, a plant will grow from each.

Care of tools

Always make sure that the garden shears are clean, dry and given a little smear of oil after use or they will become rusty and useless.

The cutting edge of shears, secateurs and so on can be sharpened with a file, but it should be done carefully so as to avoid causing damage.

Keep the blades of the lawn mower sharp, otherwise you will be tearing out the grass rather than cutting it.

Two-stroke lawn mowers can be difficult to start, the trouble usually being caused by the mixtures they run on. For easier starting, turn off the the fuel when you've finished cutting, and let the engine run to dry out the carburettor completely. Next time it should start at the first attempt.

For elderly people, particularly if they have arthritis or rheumatism, some garden chores can be difficult. If the short handles on trowels and weeding forks are replaced with ordinary broom handles it will make things much easier.

Propagation

If you run short of plastic trays to start your seeds or plants in the greenhouse or cold frame, use empty plastic margarine containers. Make a few holes in the bottom of each with a large needle and then fill up with compost in the usual way.

A little soft-bristled brush or even a small piece of fur is handy for pollinating a tree to make sure it fruits.

Protection against frost, damp and drought

Use light sacks on top of a cold frame to protect from frost. And to prevent excessive damp in a frame, a little soot or some flowers of sulphur should be mixed in with the soil.

If there is likely to be a frost late in the spring, protect the blossom on your fruit trees. Put ordinary plastic bags over the blossoms, securing each to the twig with a rubber band, and then remove them the next morning.

To keep your plants as moist as possible, put some sort of mulch round them in dry spells.

Shrubs

When planting shrubs bought from a garden centre always make a hole large enough for the soil to be mixed with damp peat before you put in the shrub.

Soil types

If you want to discover how much humus there is in your garden soil try this do-it-yourself method. Take a jamjar and fill it three-quarters full of water. Then stir two tablespoons of soil into it. If the water at the top clears rapidly with only a little humus floating at the top, the soil is sandy. If the water remains murky and there are lumps at the bottom the soil is clayey.

Translucent water with a lot of humus at the top means good soil. Incidentally, peat increases the humus content of the soil.

Car care

The engine
If the car won't start, the first thing to do is to examine the connections on the battery and starter motor. Clean them, tighten and smear with grease.

If the car breaks down and you suspect something electrical try this check. Remove a plug lead, hold it about 1/4 inch away from the engine block, then turn the engine after switching on. If there is no spark the trouble may be caused by a cracked distributor cap or a cracked rotor arm.

Always let the engine run for a couple of minutes after starting up so that oil can circulate through all the moving parts – it will make them last longer.

The windows
If you don't have any demist liquid for the car windows use a mixture of one part glycerine to six parts alcohol or methylated spirits. Keep it in a bottle for use as required. Smear it over the glass, leave for a few minutes then polish.

To prevent your windscreen frosting overnight if you don't have a garage, cover the windscreen with thick newspapers, putting them under the wipers to secure.

If you can't find the car scraper use the plastic spatula from your freezer to do the job.

If you don't have any de-icer left, make up a solution of salt and water and dab this on your windows instead, but be careful as it can corrode metal.

Upholstery
For tears in vinyl upholstery in cars get a piece of vinyl as near the original colour as possible and position it underneatn the tear. Glue it in place, pulling the edges together as much as possible.

Snags in fabric seats can be darned with a matching wool or patched as you would a household item.

95

Cleaning

When washing the car be careful not to hose the radiator as water can very easily get in. It can lie in the honeycomb grill and get into the engine when you start up.

The ideal time to wash the car is after a shower of rain. The rain will have loosened the dirt, making your job much easier.

Make sure the engine is cold before you start washing the car. A warm engine means the surface will streak.

If you have soft water then cut down on the amount of car wash or detergent you use.

A soft banister brush is ideal for cleaning the wheels of the car.

Aerials

If you have to wrestle with the car aerial to get it to move at all then give it a coat of polish at the same time as you do the car. It will then slide easily.

Emergency kit

Always carry an emergency kit in the car with you: some rags, a pair of gloves, an old blanket or doormat to kneel on and an old jacket of some kind (perhaps a thin, plastic anorak which can easily fold up small) to protect you from dirt.

The garage

Put an old tyre against the wall to act as a buffer.